Tesserae Kinned

Connecting All Australians Through the Power of Song

Maria Rosa

First published by Ultimate World Publishing 2022
Copyright © 2022 Maria Rosa

ISBN

Paperback: 978-1-922828-00-2
Ebook: 978-1-922828-01-9

Maria Rosa has asserted her rights under the Copyright, Designs and Patents Act 1988 to be identified as the author of this work. The information in this book is based on the author's experiences and opinions. The publisher specifically disclaims responsibility for any adverse consequences which may result from use of the information contained herein. Permission to use information has been sought by the author. Any breaches will be rectified in further editions of the book.

All rights reserved. No part of this publication may be reproduced, stored in or introduced into a retrieval system, or transmitted in any form, or by any means (electronic, mechanical, photocopying, recording or otherwise) without the prior written permission of the author. Any person who does any unauthorised act in relation to this publication may be liable to criminal prosecution and civil claims for damages. Enquiries should be made through the publisher.

Cover design: Ultimate World Publishing
Layout and typesetting: Ultimate World Publishing
Editor: Marinda Wilkinson

Ultimate World Publishing
Diamond Creek,
Victoria Australia 3089
www.writeabook.com.au

TESTIMONIALS

Your book is so powerful Maria – it's not just the stories. It's the way you portray them that wakes me up to the richness of this world where 'the elder who sang directly into the wind witnesses … the power of the human spirit's refusal to don the constricting and debilitating garment of victimhood and its willingness instead to enter life's challenging circumstances with dignity and deep attentiveness.' It's so beautiful to be able to witness and capture moments of voice. My teenage son also felt the powerful imagery of the elder's singing into the wind when I read it to him!

Your understandings and perspective of some of the Australian First Nations are beautiful and true. Thank you for writing your story as it links with some of theirs.

Margaret Walsh, RN, Remote Area Nurse, South Australia

Maria, I think your masterly piece of writing encapsulates many of your well-learned experiences, that began with your education and country farm teenage years followed wisely by your choice of theology training. The latter in retrospect has led to such a successful and meaningful teaching career in culturally diverse work and living environments. It has been a true privilege to read your work.

Allan Alexander,
Remote Community Worker, South Australia

PRAISE FOR
MARIA'S SONGS

Maria – this is a lifetime's work so relevant for this time. Been finding gems all morning and have so many questions ... Delighted that it was a local production ... It is world-class ... Centre of world is everywhere ...

Dr Helen Sheil, Facilitator, Director and Community Development Practitioner, Centre for Rural Communities

Fire Wrapped in Stone brings to life the soothing music and song of Maria Rosa enriched with the subtle haunting sounds of the Australian bush. Inspired by the poetry of Rod Cameron OSA, these songs remind us that, 'This is a land where every horizon sings!'[1]

Rev Dave Austin OSA, Former Provincial of the Augustinians of the Province of Australasia

Regarding the lyrics – I think the new version of 'You Are My Country' is very beautiful. On first reading I thought the sad note in: 'Bring to life within me what has been dead' might sound too sad, but on reflection, I like it, for its resurrection theme and the fact that the burning desert country is sad. (27 January 1983)

You are certainly building a bridge between Aboriginal cultures and us. (28 March 1983)

The very beautiful *Red Land Songs* have contributed richly to my ministry, especially when I give the six-day retreats and use the songs in my presentations. I have given retreats based on 'The Dreaming' and it is having a powerful appeal. Thank you for your priceless assistance. God bless. (3 April 2000)

Maria Rosa's music has both extended and released my poetry giving it 'another dimension'.

Rev Rod Cameron OSA, Intercultural Ministry Practitioner in North Queensland, Poet, Former Science Teacher at St Augustine's College, Brookvale

Meddling with magic and mystery, conjuring forgotten bones till dark and pain grow young and strong … 'seduced into childbirth' via composition, the singer becomes a song. This is Maria. Her music works to present poetry more fully and aims to convey 'story'. It is a joy to listen to – rinsing and cleansing the soul. I am welcomed by the music that she sings.

James Cornell, Poet, Songwriter and Author of 'Dark Diamond Dancing'

The songs of the album *Fire Wrapped in Stone* are characterised by peaceful tranquillity.

*Walter Shovk, Member of the
Australian Music Examiners Board*

Your music is: Sublime. Healing. Touching the universal. Among other superlatives – superb!

*Teresa and Allan Alexander,
Community Development Workers, South Australia*

Ron and I listened to your *Red Land Songs* tape Maria this weekend and very much enjoyed it. Ron was commenting that it is in a Pentatonic style (which he said was without the semitones) – to me, it sounded very 'Irish' in its rendering. Regardless, it was very beautiful and thank you for letting us share it.

Sue Trudinger, Pukatja/Ernabella, South Australia

PRAISE FOR
MARIA'S PAST WORK

Maria (is) an exemplary teacher; a scholar in Christian theology and of Indigenous thought. (She) demonstrates ecumenical respect at its best ... is equally adept within both Vocational Education and Training and Higher Education sectors, a rarity amongst theological scholars. Her research skills are of the highest standard as attested by ... her profound insight into Practical and Pastoral Theologies ... (She) brings rich life experience to the vibrant mix of cultures and languages grounded in Indigenous traditions ... a calmly forceful advocate for the needs of women, the marginalised, and those made powerless by prevailing social values.

Rev Dr Lee Levett-Olson, PhD, MDiv, BA (Hons), Grad Cert Ed, Cert IVTAE10. Educational Leader, Nungalinya College, Darwin, Northern Territory

ACKNOWLEDGEMENT OF COUNTRY

I wish to acknowledge the *Gurnai Kurnai* people from whose land I am writing. I extend my respect to their ancestors alongside their present and emerging elders. I also acknowledge with ongoing deep respect those First Peoples among whom I have been culturally immersed. I acknowledge the generous and unstinting guidance they gave me concerning their cultures, traditions and experiences. They inspired and taught me to work with them in ways respectful of their connections to the land, seas, skies, all creatures and each other. I also acknowledge their gracious hospitality to newcomers/strangers and recognise that their sovereignty has never been ceded.

Via the *Uluru Statement from the Heart*, Australian First Nations representatives reminded other Australians anew of their spiritual connection with 'the land' (as inclusive of seas and skies) and they propose a *Makarrata* springboard for forward movement. I recognise this statement addresses unfinished business in the relationship between Australia's First Nations and other Australians. On various sides of cultural divides, I acknowledge goodwill – though helpful – is not enough. Solid bridges need to be built across deep chasms created by history. Future processes followed must allow for cultural, alongside personal, differences and the mediation of these.

WARNINGS

Disclaimer: In parts of this book (which spans decades), identifiers such as names of people, locations and dates have been removed to safeguard the privacy of individuals. Expanding coincidental or perceived similarities/resemblances are thus the sole responsibility of the reader.

People descended from Australia's diverse First Nations are advised this text contains images of and references to people who have died. Triggers may be contained in the text which could activate distress. Should this happen, seeking support is recommended.

PERMISSIONS

All music (including arranging) and enclosed lyrics are protected by copyright and registered with APRA AMCOS. Should you wish to use them or any parts of them, contact APRA AMCOS for assistance in obtaining a licence from the copyright owners of the works and sound recordings:

Locked Bag 5000, Strawberry Hills NSW 2012 Australia
T: +61 2 9935 7900   E: apra@apra.com.au

The current Provincial of the Augustinians of the Province of Australasia Peter Jones OSA has permitted the inclusion of Rod Cameron OSA's 'voice' in this work, alongside Rod's personal permission given to me to use any of his work freely. This permission extends to the works by Ron Bopf OSA used. Permission to freely use James Cornell's contributions has also been received. When I interviewed Deborah Ruiz Wall and Margaret Bain on 10 September and 5 December 2005 respectively, they gave me permission to quote them directly. The photo of Rod is reprinted courtesy of the Augustinians of the Province of Australasia and the Sturt Desert Pea is courtesy of David Woods. All other photos are mine.

DEDICATION

*For Keshi who wondered if I would forget her and her people.
Your First Nation heritage is a gift
to all Australians
and the global community.*[2]

For my and Keis' parents with a bursting, grateful heart.

*For all those First Peoples who
'grew me up' according to their ways.*[3]

*For those beautiful souls I have met
who have genuinely 'heard'
my search for transformative praxis
attentive to healing and reconciliation.*

CONTENTS

PROLOGUE	1
INTRODUCTION: SINGING INTO THE WIND	11
CHAPTER 1: SINGING IN THE SUN	25
CHAPTER 2: SINGING SILENCE	41
CHAPTER 3: CIRCA KING SOUND	59
CHAPTER 4: WELCOMING PRESENCE	69
CHAPTER 5: 'STORYING'	89
CHAPTER 6: 'NOT FAR FROM OODNADATTA'	109
CHAPTER 7: BEYOND 'TINSEL' BINARIES	117
CHAPTER 8: 'HARVEST HAPPINESS'	131
CHAPTER 9: INTERDEPENDENTLY 'KINNED'	145
CHAPTER 10: STILLING TERROR OF LOSS	159
AFTERWORD	173
ABOUT THE AUTHOR	181
FURTHER ACKNOWLEDGEMENTS	187
REFERENCES & NOTES	193

PROLOGUE

Listen, O drop, give yourself up without regret,
and in exchange gain the Ocean.
Listen, O drop, bestow upon yourself this honor,
And in the arms of the Sea be secure.
……………………
Give a drop, and take this Sea full of pearls.

Rumi[1]

Isabel Allende's words, 'Write what should not be forgotten' speak to me of experiences in the contexts in which I have found myself. My encounters with First Nations people in Australia and elsewhere are among those not to be forgotten. They strongly reside at the core of my sense of belonging in Australia and knowing that 'The human soul is a citizen of the Universe.'[2] Antoine de Saint-Exupéry's poetic words also resonate: 'To travel, above all, is to change one's skin.'[3] For me, this includes 'travelling' within other cultures.

Keshi, to whom I have dedicated this book, asked as I prepared to leave her community, 'Are you going to forget about us, Maria?'

My heart leapt into my mouth on hearing this question and I found myself answering with another: 'How could that ever happen?'

Many experiences connected with her people and others of Australian First Nations heritage will not appear in writing, yet they continue to live in my heart. They are a source of joy and gratitude. I can truly say that with the First Nations people I have encountered, I have adventured into this wondrous land and further – into the very heart of humanity.

Keshi, this book is a testament to the fact I have forgotten neither you nor your people nor the many others of First Nations descent who have graced my being on this continent and elsewhere. We all have to make difficult decisions in our lives and leaving your community proved to be one of the hardest. Yet, I know that who and what we value become part of us and live within the very tissue and texture of our souls. No-one can dismantle the essence of this tissue nor the nuanced exquisite nature of its eternally sacred beauty. This reality can ultimately live and supersede process outcomes such as, for example, the Northern Territory National Emergency Response (NTNER) aka 'The Intervention'.

To avoid misunderstanding, it is important at this juncture I formally situate myself. I am not a person of Australian First Nations lineage and I do not speak for them. Amid their diversity, I have sought to grow with their guidance to become a better human being and grow into a greater understanding of their perspectives. Thus, while these pages cannot help but reveal the product of some of this educational process, it is necessary to recognise all people – whether of First Nations heritage or not – speak from within their particular context. Indeed, I have heard some people of our First Nations carefully and explicitly underline the fact they cannot and will not speak for people of other First

Nations regarding certain matters. This is despite the expectations of other Australians.

When I approached an elected First Nations Councillor thinking what I needed to raise came under his area of responsibility, he gently redirected me: 'Maria, you will need to talk with the traditional custodian about that one. The traditional custodian for that country is my wife.' This simple exchange challenged my previous enculturation and conditionings. Vicariously as a woman, I found it liberating to meet incarnational affirmation that women functioned equally in the traditional realm in that community. Women of First Nations descent – at times described around the world as 'Indigenous' – have often found themselves twice marginalised, via seemingly 'cavalier' perceptions and practices operating within both mainstream and church patriarchy/hierarchies. Indeed, the theologian Elisabeth Schüssler Fiorenza asks us to consider examining the status quo from the theory of 'kyriarchy'.[4]

Attributing motive is an area of strong hesitancy among First Nations people with whom I have lived. This speaks to me of efforts to truly live with integrity. For how can we know or intuit fully the mind of another? To me, this is an example of living fairly – showing respect by allowing others first and foremost to speak for themselves.

This text essentially accompanies a musical memoir: my songs. The songs grew from my journeying in the intercultural field where Australian First Peoples understandings and ways of being meet those of other Australians. Until formally allocated a place within a kinship system, my being an 'outsider' remained the status quo. To assist the local members of several communities, I accepted the invitation to fill roles with parameters primarily defined by the dominant 'Anglo' culture. However, community members still strongly asserted their decision-making powers within mainstream processes – even via quiet resistance. Over the years, I found myself asking more and more difficult questions and recognising the value of customising engagement efforts so these explicitly acknowledged elements within the local context and particular ways of being. Suspending judgement shaped by mainstream thinking proved a valuable standard practice while navigating situations where various cultures engage.

Many of my questions started and became deeply serious after seeing appalling living conditions and especially high suicide rates. I continually searched inside myself for reconciliation between realities discovered and those pervading mainstream institutional thought. I asked myself questions like: Where am I being asked to collude with something that is ultimately corrosive? How do existing mainstream systems contribute to the status quo? What happens when some holders of mainstream positions claim meetings are a 'waste of time' when Indigenous 'issues' are raised? How is cultural safety created for all? When and how is adequate decision-making power able to be exercised by people of Indigenous descent about that which impacts their lives? What do we do when we notice First Nations people having to enter a pub (public house licensed to sell alcohol) via a different entrance?

Thankfully, some elements of local situations have changed over the past five decades. Thus, we can breathe a sigh of relief, while hanging on to the hope that all will continue to improve. The Augustinian Rod Cameron concluded:

> The rocky road was far too long,
> The shadows were too deep
> ……..
> Their lonely fires are flickering low
> Their Sacred Dream was dim.
> ……..

PROLOGUE

> But there is a brilliant ring of hope
> Around the silvery moon.[5]

Yet the memory of finding 'KKK' sprayed on the double corrugated iron gates of a service station's yard, carved on a tree along a morning walk and etched in the sand on a pathway, remains in my mind's eye, among other images collected over the years. No wonder First Nations people with whom I worked at the time told me they were frightened to go to town. A magistrate not of Indigenous descent also had 'KKK' painted on his garage door in a New South Wales town.[6] Another question therefore arises: How do we, as bystanders, seek to safely, and using our particular gifts, counter such intimidation? Given that 'Silence in the face of injustice is complicity with the oppressor'?[7] And, in the end, people remember not the words of their enemies, but the silence of their friends?[8]

Many I have had the privilege of knowing and learning from have died. Their names will always live in my heart, if not here in print. Out of respect for their living relatives, I refrain from naming them and have removed identifiers. Some already stand in the public domain, even after their deaths. Sister Agatha *Midaringi* FDNSC, for example, has been mentioned in a public forum since her death in 1984.[9] Some people from whom I sought knowledge are happy to be more widely known while others are not. These personal and cultural preferences have been, and will continue to be, respected.

Neither Rod Cameron nor James Cornell, whose words I use directly as lyrics or inspiring sources for my songwriting, is of Australian First Nations descent. They, like myself, have been born in the land now known as 'Australia'. Somehow, we all ended up spending significant time in the intercultural fields mentioned and being immensely blessed by, as well as challenged, within them. We all also had the privilege of being able to study overseas, discover broader frames of reference and return to our country enriched. May you find the works included in this text instrumental in assisting you to discover what being a citizen of your country, and the Universe, means in your life adventure of negotiating the 'secular' and the 'sacred'. Do you see a division between them? If so, where do the differentiations lie?

In these limited number of pages, I am only documenting parts of my musical memoir with a small number of the many elements pertinent to the contexts in which I wrote the songs. I cannot include, reference, exhaust or respond to all the voices who have attended to dimensions of these fields of endeavour over the years. Most definitively, do not expect this text to be a standard academic treatise. Nowhere does what I write here comprehensively cover the composition of all contexts. What I have written is merely a stroke on a much bigger canvas that many others, including myself, have intentionally engaged. I cannot possibly include all their voices and therefore this text cannot be used to arrive at simplistic analyses or assessments of any context. A text will always be limited if we only seek satisfactory answers to our questions while ignoring others. This text asserts many voices are currently absent or consistently erased from relevant discourses.

My contact with those of Australian First Nations heritage began in earnest not long after State Shipping Services ceased carrying passengers in Western Australia. Since then, I have learned as much as possible about our First Peoples. There is always more growth open to us as Australians. I urge you to find and seek what is needed to create transformative healing and reconciliation. I know assumptions made about others without a fuller knowledge of their contexts and intentions can mislead. That is why many First Nations Australians I know intentionally tend to work within a formal acknowledgment of the many interconnecting elements.

They attend to the culturally-based perspectives of others to inform themselves while safeguarding their sovereignty and holding their meaningful identity.

It is all too easy for unowned and unprocessed parts of ourselves to be projected onto these individuals and groups. In coming to an informed position as an Australian operating solely within the mainstream, therefore, we need to at least develop a degree of tolerance for ambiguity and differing modes of learning. Otherwise, it is easy to fall into the trap of misinterpreting what is happening, assigning motives that do not do justice to others and being accusatory. In coming to helpful decision-making together, we need to engage in a process where current judgements become suspended to gain context-relevant data. Deep attention needs to be applied which increases education, so what we learn is brought into dialogue with previous understandings. There is too much at stake to rigidly enforce monocultural paradigms we have unconsciously imbibed.

For me, there is no substitute for cultural immersion, being willing to go through the process of attending at some stage to being as a child within other cultural ways, speaking with those of First Nations heritage with deep levels of attentiveness or reading their works. In cultural immersion, we can choose to either be enriched, extended or battened down in defensive isolation.

This text is no substitute for reading the many other authors who, as a result of thoughtful open engagement in the field, share some aspects of deep knowledge-exchanging encounters with First Nations people and others spread over many years. There is no single Aboriginal and Torres Strait Islander culture and any attempts to generalise in the interest of creating one to resolve the tension caused by differences need to be viewed carefully. We also need to hold a hermeneutic of suspicion about ourselves in tension with presenting perspectives. Contexts matter. Indeed, the level of diversity one meets can be breathtaking. There is danger in both generalising the particular and particularising the general in any intercultural context as these prevent deep listening.

In this field of exchange, there is no substitute for building safe 'level' (horizontal) culturally enlightened relationships as distinct from top-down (vertical) ones.[10] To do so, we need to become aware that not all conversational styles are the same, and time to allow for these to fully achieve their intended purpose needs to be considered. To obtain depth and authenticity, lifelong research and study are important. We need to persist over time to learn within developing, trusting relationships. It is helpful to remember not every First Nations person automatically operates biculturally in the 'Anglo' mainstream and the same applies to other Australians entering First Nations cultural spaces. We are still on a learning journey together.

Finding what will work in particular contemporary contexts requires participation at all levels by First Nations people who are impacted by dominant mainstream thought. The present can be and needs to be briefed by the past as the latter contributes to the underlying shape of the present. Registering 'the extreme urgency of the environmental crisis and his long-held belief in time, patience and the careful observation of other cultures as the basis for the fix', Barry Lopez asserts: 'As time grows short, the necessity to listen to foundational stories other than our own becomes imperative.'[11] The present grants us new possibilities to move through realities contoured by the past. To live more fully in tandem with First Peoples in the present will enable the creation of a life-enhancing future for all. Reading this text can thus only be an invitational stepping stone offered along your journey. It invites you to meditatively listen to

PROLOGUE

and experience the music available via the website https://www.singinghorizonsrosa.com. Each song's album is listed in the Notes section at the end of the book.

May the songs and this text prompt you both as a listener and attentive reader to ask more questions of your own and societies' generalising metanarratives.

Capturing a desert mood

INTRODUCTION

SINGING INTO THE WIND

'But deepest Dreams are born of darkest nights.'

Rod Cameron

An elder stood at a small open church window to the side of an altar as the tropical cyclone approached. He sang into the darkening sky. Earlier that day community members received a warning to shelter in case of flying debris and other risks. So, we gathered in the church, a strong brick building thought to be the best construction in the community for withstanding cyclonic force winds. With pews pushed to one side, blankets stretched out on the floor, the confessional converted into a latrine for emergency use, we waited. Bubbles of uncertainty filled the air like holes in Swiss cheese as predictions about cyclonic behaviours are not totally reliable. Rain fell torrentially, and gale winds howled. According to a previous communication, the eye of the cyclone would miss us but that forecast had since changed. Peering through the main door, I could see the water level outside rising. Somehow, this elder's singing felt soothing, emanating hope the forces of nature may relent or once again change direction, soften their fury or intent if they listened to this human voice touching them through song. Unprotected by glass panes, the words musically released into the open air seemed to unflinchingly look reality in the eye before swirling and falling like windblown petal confetti.

Remembering the above incident, I realise how over the years I have used the metaphor of a storm in my songs to capture the disaster-creating forces which bore down on the peoples of Australia's First Nations from the late eighteenth century. This metaphorical and damaging 'storm' began when others from across the sea came to 'camp' permanently. They claimed the land as theirs to do with as they wished. Unlike in *Aotearoa*/New Zealand and some other colonised places, no overarching formal treaty emerged over time with the local inhabitants. Practically, the British flag flew high for decades with the mantra *terra nullius* firmly 'sung' into its cloth and stitching. The ferocious winds and lashing rains of the 'storm' thus unleashed altered the original inhabitants' ability to structure their own lives according to patterns of living knowledge fledged over thousands of years.

Ultimately, just as we could not lightly dismiss the warnings sent regarding this cyclone, the original inhabitants of this land could not ignore a threat of the magnitude posed by the newcomers. All held dear – indeed the very lives of people who saw strangers land and set off to grasp promises of fortunes in the hinterland – faced imminent death. The elder singing into the wind symbolises for me all those voices which have, since the late 1700s, attempted to speak truthfully to the life-threatening forces of colonisation, to seek negotiated understandings of its consequences for the First Peoples. Through exploding and imploding impacts, they expressed hope of being 'heard'. Concerted efforts of many survivors recently produced the *Uluru Statement from the Heart* in this perennial hope.[1]

'Black December'

One of my responses via song to a critical, destructive incident occurred over forty years ago. A friend from a community where I had lived saved enough money to bring her niece and herself to the city for a holiday. We had been looking forward to spending time together, seeing the many unique sights one can enjoy. Conscious of how dwarfed I felt standing amid the imposing high-rise buildings of the Central Business District soon after leaving their community, I had carefully planned our vacation itinerary. Accommodation-wise, we shared a homely set-up. However, a fatal incident back in the community compelled abandonment of our plans. After only three days, I farewelled them at the airport. I then wrote a song to help me process what had happened. The imagery of a storm build up focused my efforts to absorb the incident's impact and make sense of the life-extinguishing violence touching our lives' flow.

Unfortunately, much is often made in the media about violence in remote Australian locations where the population is predominantly of First Nations and hybrid descent. The sad reality is that behavioural violence is ubiquitous in Australia, not only confined to these contexts – and, even systemic. Where tendencies towards the use of violence are kept sufficiently in check, I have learned life has its best chance to flourish, calibrate its life-enhancing level, and negotiate for fairness or understanding – even when differing perspectives clash. One of the overwhelming difficulties, however, is that many do not realise how their unexamined so-called 'natural' behaviour impacts others. The cultural systems from which their expectations interpret and unconsciously attribute absolutism to their viewpoints can be experienced as oppressive by those living from vastly different cultural frameworks.

Just as storm clouds build up pressure in the atmosphere, pressure builds in relationships via the insistence of the 'rightness' of one way over another. When such pressure erupts without proactive sensitive address or preparation to compromise on all sides or careful consensus-building in contexts where cultures or differing personalities meet, the people whose reality is denied become trapped *'like fish in a net'*. I have heard other Australians in several contexts involving First Peoples remark: 'It (the eruption of violence) just came out of nowhere!!!' Very often, however, if we are familiar with the context, its current dynamics, and already attuned to seeing from within another cultural perspective, we may have been able to discern warning signs triggered by the pressures of repeated microaggressions and being misunderstood.

Taking the time to check out what is being seen and felt outside our cultural perspective, we may become familiar with and enlightened via the contours created by microaggressions continually experienced by others. Sometimes mind games including gaslighting can be played in the assertion of one way of being over another. These impact health, triggering lateral violence, particularly where unreflective power differentials strongly exist. Although First Nations people resisted the onslaught of mainstream cultural ways, hardcore power differentials asserted themselves via the east of the continent from 1788 onwards. These often are unconsciously (as well as consciously) reasserted as 'The Way' to be. One valid question I learned to keep asking myself in such contexts is: 'How much "swallowing" is going on and by whom?'

Here are the lyrics of 'Black December' written as I absorbed and processed the genesis and impact of the violence directed towards my friend's sister. (Throughout this text, the lyrics of songs recorded will be shared in a similar format. To hear the melodies, harmonies and soundscapes, or to purchase the song, visit https://www.singinghorizonsrosa.com/.)

BLACK DECEMBER

They came from afar
The door to their heart still left ajar
Over months they had planned
While heart horizons I scanned
It was good to see them again.

But then came the pain
Only after three days
They departed
A violent fight
Left them broken-hearted.

Like storm clouds of the Wet
Trapping people like fish in a net
Violence descended on Claire
Decreeing she could no more be there.

No here she could no longer be
Her spirit now in her country
She cries to us through others' eyes
Grows silent if their flame dies.

Black December, touched in blood red
Gold of freedom be your daily bread

Black December, red and gold
Can steel you from your foe.
Red and gold cannot be sold
Be brave, be bold, be daring
Your freedom lies in your still caring.

Let no one dim her star,
Let no one dim her star.

Lyrics and Music: Maria Rosa

The mention of the colours red, black and gold in the lyrics alludes to the assertion of realities perpetrated by the first lie: *terra nullius*. These colours are incorporated in the Aboriginal flag, a symbol of the enduring strength of First Nations peoples and their ongoing spiritual connection with the land.[2]

Spirit Connection

While studying 'The Spirituality of Lakota-Christian Dialogue' in the United States, I viewed a film titled *Where the Spirit Lives*.[3] This is an excellent – if chilling – portrayal of the consequences when people adjust, adjust and readjust to colonisation until who they are is threatened with disappearance. In repeatedly giving in to the demand for 'adjustment', they effectively 'swallow' who they are. Via the tailoring which occurs when only others' cultural expectations and expressions are given privileged value, they become a carbon copy of others. The status quo can existentially become intolerable and is an example of the extension of 'an iron fist in a velvet glove' resting on their shoulder. Though set in Canada, we can find echoes in the film of the experiences of First Nations elsewhere.

After the viewing, some questions arose for me. Is an education delivered without acknowledging the value of existing First Nations cultural frameworks and the need to respect them, simply training them to permanently wear invisibility cloaks for the convenience and expectations of those living the officially 'better' culture? And, if (as Frances Clark says), 'There is music in every child. The teacher's job is to find it and nurture it', what is being asked of a teacher in intercultural praxis? The embrace of red, black and gold insists *terra nullius* is a dying fiction and, from this fact, more clarifying questions flow.

Upon the death of one of my colleagues, some 'Kiwis' (natives of *Aotearoa*/New Zealand) performed a love-filled ceremony outside the building where he had lived. They shared that 'The recently dead are released into the care of the long-dead.' They spoke of restoring the *tapu*, the sacredness of place: '*Māori* restore *tapu* sacredness by *Karakia* prayer. *Wairua* is an integral part of *tapu*. *Karakia* embraces all those present and not present.'[4] Writing a song about Claire's death made sense to me in a way similar to how *Māori* describe the restoration of *tapu*. It acknowledged the sacredness of her spirit and that within all lives suddenly and violently cut short.

When tragedy happens through lateral violence in communities, I learned to ask: 'What are the unhealed issues?' Asking this question does not automatically condone any violence but seeks to face the pain expressed and its sources. Here is one explanation:

> Lateral violence – also called internalised colonialism or horizontal violence – happens when people who have been oppressed for a long time feel so powerless that rather than fighting back against their oppressor, they unleash their fear, anger and frustration against their own community members. For Indigenous communities,

> lateral violence is a part of a larger cycle of hurt that has its roots in colonisation, trauma, racism and discrimination.
>
> Sometimes those who hurt others with lateral violence may not be 100% aware of their actions or the suffering their actions cause. This might be because lateral violence often provides individuals who hurt others with a false sense of power or influence.[5]

It may be helpful to ask, for example, when violence erupts 'out of nowhere': Is this an example of lateral violence? What is not being addressed? How are people being treated and processes enacted? Who or what is being excluded? Is there a unique conversational event like the *Yankunytjatjara aalpiri* available for the airing of grievances? 'Yankunytjatjara people from Central Australia gave a regular *aalpiri*, early in the morning as people are beginning to gather around their campfires. The older people walk around the camp, loudly speaking about matters of public importance and complaining about their grievances. Just as there is no equivalent speech event to *aalpiri* in western societies, there is no *interview* in traditional Aboriginal societies.'[6]

Any unfinished business may present as needing attention through the medium of lateral violence. 'It is a truism that the past is never past in the repeating cycles of colonial injustices. The past reappears "always to rupture the present" and the ghosts of the dead clamour for a reckoning.'[7] In analysing such situations, Christians may speak of an individual's conscious giving into defect/transgression/missing the mark (as 'personal sin') and harmful inherited/transmitted patterns followed uncritically ('original sin' and 'social/structural sin'). *Alpech* clansman Tyson Yunkaporta speaks of the need to keep the spirit in balance and hold 'in check the shadow of the I-am-greater-than deception'.[8]

A formal attempt addressing the 'clamour for a reckoning' societally in Australia occurred via the formation of the Council of Aboriginal Reconciliation with unanimous cross-party support in 1995. It established a network of Australians for Reconciliation coordinators which helped grassroots communities explore relevant issues. With the election of the Federal Government led by Prime Minister John Howard, the policy of 'Practical Reconciliation' formally entered the political arena. Without making judgements about the character of specific individuals and yet not exempting them from valid personal responsibility, it is helpful to distil possible future insights by recognising societal context and its component elements. We can be further challenged when living in unfamiliar contexts by leaning into questions, searching for patterns in observations and standard 'stale' interpretations of happenings.

One tool used at times by anthropologists is participant observation. It is one I recommend as helpful for distancing self to see a bigger picture or recognise when our interpretations may need further local input. It can also, accompanied by honesty and humility, help us get in touch with absolutism connected with our cultural biases. It greatly assists journeying through culture shock and reverse culture shock – realities often dismissed when entering and exiting immersion in remote and very remote communities where most inhabitants are of Indigenous descent. However, this tool demands discipline. Deborah Ruiz Walls adopts Raimon/Raimundo Panikkar's idea of 'cultural disarmament' as her starting point to facilitate intercultural liberating practice.[9] Participant observation will assist with what she says Panikkar describes as getting out of 'the trenches' in which 'modern culture' of 'western origin' has dug in, surrounded by vested and non-negotiable values such as progress, technology, science, democracy and the world market.[10]

Songs in the Fluidity Between the Past and the Present

Describing his experience of Cyclone Tracy, Peter Spillett, a survivor of the bombing of London and the Burma campaign said it was 'the most traumatic experience' he had ever had.[11] The author of *Warning* (a book about this event) wrote:

> When Law is sung in Indigenous songs it becomes a way of structuring and interpreting knowledge as well as communicating it. Boundaries between the past and present are fluid and while references will be able to establish a rough time period – 'That horse and buggy time'[12] – a chronology is less relevant than remembering events in a way that emphasises their meaning. An extension is what Deborah Rose has described as 'Year Zero'[13]: the moment something irrevocably shifts in a culture. For Indigenous people, 'Year Zero' is white settlement.

Indeed, this 'Year Zero' in hindsight can be said to be the equivalent of them surviving the damage caused by a cyclone of the highest possible intensity. When I visited Berlin, I saw the vibrancy of Australian Indigenous art in the *Traumzeit* exhibition and the contents of that city's restored *Die Neue Synagoge* which had been destroyed during World War (WW) II. For me, they underlined the reality of victory for Indigenous and Jewish people over adversity (aka the 'storms' which beset and leave human beings bereft of so much). Perhaps WWII itself and the destruction it brought to many people's lives could be described as a 'Year Zero' that irrevocably shifted something in the cultures of many. The refugee Behrouz Boochani expresses one such shift: 'The collective trauma from the journey is in our veins – each of those boat odysseys founded a new imagined nation.'[14]

A person who saw evidence of such victory among Australia's First Peoples is Rod Cameron OSA. I met him serendipitously six years after he had inspired me via the content of his poetry to continue investing creatively in the storytelling power of music. Recently, a person called the songs I have composed and sung over time 'a musical memoir'. Indeed, I had not seen them that way before but, once she said it, I recognised this to be true. The songs are tools I have used to prompt processing and reflection on encounters spread over decades.

My songs can be called signposts of meaning-making along a way in which many people of Indigenous descent and I accompanied each other. The songs grew in varying contexts and I use them here to communicate a mere smattering of the knowledge I gained after leaving Victoria and travelling interstate with two girlfriends. I did so in response to a picture of a young person of Indigenous descent in obvious poor health sent to me with an invitation 'to work on a grey, desolate marshland'. Despite some of the startling circumstances which greeted me on this journey, the elder who sang directly into the wind witnessed for me the power of the human spirit's refusal to don the constricting and debilitating garment of victimhood and its willingness to enter life's challenging circumstances with dignity and deep attentiveness.

In seeking to capture the different emphases in paths chosen as distinct from victimhood, William (Bill) H Edwards (a former Methodist and later Uniting Church Minister on the *Anangu Pitjantjatjara Yankunytjatjara* Lands in the northwest of South Australia) made the following thought-provoking general comparison between the First Nations among whom he worked for decades and many other Australians. He asserted those with European origins defined themselves as, 'I think therefore I am', whereas the First Australians ascribed more compellingly to *Canto ergo sum* ('I sing therefore I am').[15] Notably, a line in the *Yolŋu* language of northeast Arnhem Land: *Wä ngam ngarra marrtji buma ngarra dhuwal* assertively proclaims: 'I create different places as I travel' – as distinct from 'Travel creates a different me.' This *Yolŋu* text speaks particularly to creativity inherent within the intertwining of being and singing.[16]

Writing songs has been part of my living more fully into the encounter between older and newer ways of being in the cultural meeting spaces between First Nations peoples and others. Whenever life threw my father a formidable curveball, he inevitably ended up in song. He had faced death many times during WWII, and spoke in hushed tones at distinct times of the horrific bombings and the ensuing chaos he saw as he fled a German concentration camp liberated by American troops. I sing the following words sagely penned by Rod Cameron regarding uncertain times. They speak to the dreams of many elders which, through uncontrollable circumstances, may seem to have disappeared only to resurrect anew.

ODE TO YOUTH: THE OLD AND THE NEW

1. *The dreams of the old man dissolve in the rain,*
   But comes the young lover who dreams them again.

2. *New morning is touching the crest of the hill.*
   The songs that were silenced are echoing still.

3. *The past and the present in ritual wed.*
   Give birth to the future. The Dream is not dead.

4. *The food of encounter puts flesh on the bone.*
   That culture is feeble that lives on its own.

5. *When thoughts are compounded, they blaze from the heart.*
   Ideals that are blended are pregnant with art.

6. *So let the flames mingle, let camp-fires unite,*
   Young eyes that are shining have captured the light.
   Young eyes that are shining have captured the light.

7. *The dreams of the old man dissolve in the rain,*
   But comes the young lover who dreams them again.
   Who dreams them again.

> *Lyrics: Rod Cameron, 27 September 1992*
> *Music: Maria Rosa*

'A red land sings in the sun'

CHAPTER 1

SINGING IN THE SUN

I WALK BY NIGHT
*(Alternate name: **NOT ALONE**)*

Again, I walk by night but not alone,
Humanity treads this moonlit grass with me,
By reaching I can touch, the friendly hands.

The one-eyed windmill standing wide awake,
In muttering labour blades the spacious air,
While I stand gazing out at spiralled galaxies.

Out there are other windmills watching too,
Waiting for the separates to meet,
Each lonely in the night,
But not alone.

Lyrics: Rod Cameron
Music: Maria Rosa

At a concert in Innisfail in 1987, Rod introduced the above song thus:

> The first poem I shall read and the first song relate to solitude, walking by night. This resulted from my experience of walking outside at Beagle Bay in the far northwest of Western Australia, in the Kimberley region. I was walking by night in this lonely place and, across the sky – the moonless sky, I noted a canopy of stars. On the hill, I could see a windmill slowly turning in the night and I became extremely conscious of profound loneliness and solitude in this lonely land. But my experience was such that I came to believe the experience of loneliness is a doorway to humanity. A person who has experienced extreme loneliness can find that to be a doorway to human communication. You realise what friendship means when you have at some time experienced loneliness extremely. It is truly a doorway to humanity. Many can find themselves in front of this doorway.[1]

People can live solitarily, away from other community members in any location. However, those who work deeply in the intercultural field of 'remote' communities peopled predominantly by First Australians do find themselves in front of a doorway to greater humanity. The latter occurs through meeting challenging diversity at this doorway, not simply loneliness. Experiences may speak of the power evidenced through developing and maintaining trusting relationships in co-designing and achieving outcomes despite distance-creating cultural differences. The land on which remote and very remote communities are found is often not only geographically distant from the context of the majority of other Australians but also often marginal to the latter's existence and understanding. In 2006, 69% of non-Indigenous Australians lived in major cities.[2] When some First Australians speak of the land as 'lonely', they seem to also reference an alienation from being understood and accepted, suggesting previous caring human relationships which sustained the nature of the land are now missing or lost. The land is related to as a subject not an object.

Ngarlun Burr/Beagle Bay

In terms of its isolation relative to major cities, Beagle Bay can be thought of as a 'lonely place'. Years ago, the tropical Wet closed access to it via the then unsealed Broome Cape Leveque Road composed of corrugated *pindan* soil.[3] Locally the site of Beagle Bay is called *Ngarlun Burr* yet, in many narratives, this fact has in the past been omitted. European history informs us that Trappist monks established the present community site around 1890 and, over time, it became one of the places where children who had been stolen from their parents because of government policies resided. Loneliness experienced without the tangible love of their parents would undoubtedly have been palpable at times in this place of transplantation, strangeness and homesickness. Many would not have realised that failing to acknowledge the traditional name of this place could evidence a measure of the erasure of much previously found to be nourishing. It is reported the mission 'was also reluctantly used as a reform school for "wayward" girls'.[4] Kathy Watson, removed from a leprosarium in Derby, however, recalls being very happy there with her mother-figure May Howard as well as 'with the good Sisters of St John of God and the Pallottine priests'.[5] Some experiences have not been so positive in outcome.[6]

Before one Wet hit, I accompanied some students who had been attending school elsewhere back home to Beagle Bay (as it was generally called back then) and Lombadina for the Christmas holiday break. The rustic bush Lombadina church struck me then as a most appropriate place to celebrate the simplicity I associate with Christmas.[7] During my stay, I observed great restlessness among the youth and mooted the value of having locally-based holiday activities.

No-one I heard spoke openly then of traditional names. However, Lombadina/Lombardina seems to have been adapted from the *Bardi Loombarrdina*, 'The area where Jilirr creek enters the sea. At some point, however, it seems to have been etymologised as "Little Lombardy".'[8] Now, more accept and are prepared to acknowledge Australia had a rich human history of occupation before the arrival of the British tall ships and, alluding to these traditional names, can even be viewed favourably. The proclamation by Governor Bourke on 10 October 1835, implementing the doctrine of *terra nullius* was incorrect; legally, the principles thus enshrined only changed in 1992 via a decision of the High Court of Australia related to the case of Eddie Mabo.[9]

Effectively, the proclamation of *terra nullius* meant the denial of what was real and important to First Peoples – the very existence of their foundational understandings and validity of the mechanisms through which they attributed meaning to life. Thus, systemically, the majority of other Australians for a long time have unconsciously participated in a legal fiction that subjugated the ultimate concerns and decision-making power of its First Peoples and privileged their own. Although Aboriginal men in South Australia could vote after the passing of the South Australian constitution in 1856 and technically Aboriginal women in that state could vote from 1894, in some cases, they were actively discouraged from enrolling and doing so. After the 1902 *Commonwealth Franchise Act* removed Aboriginal and Torres Strait Islanders' right to vote, this right was only reinstated in 1962.[10]

We are now still seeing some visible social shifts, albeit slowly, premised on a budding acknowledgement of the previous occupation of this country for millennia. There is now even the occasional bilingual sign announcing entry to and acknowledging a locale's previous name. Having also visited *Ngarlun Burr*/Beagle Bay, I can imagine Rod Cameron walking in that landscape and being struck by the significance of quality relationships where the realities of others are recognised in friendship; where, while *'waiting for the separates to meet'*, each is *'lonely in the night'* but through the gift of friendship and developing understanding, they can become *'not alone'*. The song is a call to valuing friendship as a doorway for our entry into a deeper, nuanced way of expressing our common humanity – one in which no Australian's reality or experience is isolated or gaslit out of existence.

Cheeky/Bad/Dangerous Spirits

Many years ago in a hostel, boarding schoolchildren from the *Ngarlun Burr-Loombarrdina* area and elsewhere shared their fear of 'The Red Dress Lady'. When I asked them to tell me more about her and why she was so scary, they replied she wandered around at night, kidnapping and eating children. I still do not know the origin of this story even though I tried to track it down. Had she been introduced to keep active children quiet and together at night? As they fearfully whispered of her, it reminded me of stories like Hansel and Gretel in which children are portrayed as at genuine risk. I do not know if 'The Red Dress Lady' is still active after so long or whether her story/character has changed over time. Her presence in 'mind' then may have been the result of a syncretic process influenced by common attitudes to the 'wayward' girls previously mentioned. She does feature in a recent book written in an Indigenous language I hear.[11]

One night with a different cohort elsewhere, some students would not sleep in their tents. They gathered around the campfire saying evil spirits wandered the night. The spirits were *cheeky*. I have heard *Pitjantjatjara* and *Yankunytjatjara* speakers describe such spirits as *mamu*. 'They are generally invisible, and more dangerous at night, but can be seen by dogs and more experienced older people.'[12] In Aboriginal English, *cheeky* can refer to dangerous behaviour – people can speak of a dog or snake for example as *cheeky*. I felt inspired over time to compose music for the following lullaby.

REST – A LULLABY

Rest, my young one, rest.
Let gentle night fall, heal the hurts of the past.
Drift into dreams
That wipe the harms away.

Sleep, my young one, sleep.
See how the sun goes down to sleep
In its last honey light.
See how the stars come forth like friends
In the gentleness of night.

Dream, my young one, dream,
Of a bright new world
That will come at morning time.
The shadows of the past will fade away
And new hope will shine.

Lyrics: Rod Cameron
Music: Maria Rosa

Fellowship with the Stars

Leading up to one Easter, I received an invitation to accompany a colleague on another visit to *Ngarlun Burr*/Beagle Bay. With some locals there, we spent a whole day exploring one of the offshore islands. Without realising the passing of time, we found ourselves leaving the island in the dark. However, none of the locals seemed concerned. They simply navigated by the stars and we smoothly returned to *Ngarlun Burr*/Beagle Bay. Out at sea on a boat in the dark under a cloudless sky proved to be a magical, awe-inspiring experience. The stars' reflections moved with the waves and danced in the wake behind the craft. Truly, I found it no surprise to discover the following poem which Rod Cameron wrote in 1991:

> Human life is lived in two dimensions.
> One out-stretches to the long horizons
> While the other gives us fellowship with the stars,
> One is secular and the other is sacred.
>
> The secular and the sacred need each other
>
> We leave our footprints on the crimson earth
> And light our little campfires in the night
> But our human spirit cannot be contained.
> It leaps beyond the canopy of stars.
>
> The human soul is a citizen of the Universe.

Becoming more familiar with Rod's writings, we realise his spirit did not stay contained solely by the known. As a scientist, he sought beyond it and, via a scientifically trained mind, came to understand the perspective of the First Peoples he met. He moved beyond any divisions and distortions promulgated by culturally-based categorisations to encounter others within their realities and created a safe space in which an authentic relationship could gently develop. From within that relationship, he came to an understanding that some resonances and echoes of his grasp of the spiritual journey – despite its cultural frameworks – existed within theirs. Those who knew him and are familiar with the Augustinian ideals of community, friendship and hospitality can say that he lived them as he travelled this vast land and recognised how First Peoples fostered them too through their ways.[13]

The Known and Unknown

As we have seen, Rod understood each human being as a citizen of the Universe, a being capable of fellowship with the stars, the 'secular and the sacred'. In their seminal work *Emu Dreaming: An Introduction to Australian Aboriginal Astronomy*, accomplished husband and wife team Ray and Cilla Norris underline this too. They tell us of their meeting with *Mathulu Munyarryun*, the *Yolngu* ceremonial leader and custodian of the ancient stories of the sky in the remote community of *Dhalinybuy* in northeast Arnhem Land. Searching to understand how Indigenous Australians have related to the skies, they felt honoured to meet *Mathulu* as the custodian of the 'Evening Star story' – distinct from the tales of Venus as the Morning Star. Through this meeting, they learn of an error in the anthropology books they had read. They alert us to the dark patches and channels within the Milky Way where there 'are clouds of dust in which new stars are born'.[14] They acknowledge: 'Our European ancestors explained the pattern of the stars in terms of constellations of Greek gods. The Aboriginal people living in Australia thousands of years ago also interpreted these patterns, but with a difference. Whereas the Europeans saw only the pattern in stars, the Aboriginal people also saw meaning in the dark patches.'[15]

Here we have an example of the value of linking with and listening to members of First Peoples who are THE sources of their ancient knowledge. Some people who immerse themselves in such learning say they find their world upended. Moving outside their comfort zones changed their perspectives. In describing this formative process for his band, Midnight Oil's frontman Peter Garrett said: 'We sorta had our DNA configured.'[16] I find resonances of my own experiences in such attempts to describe this adventure. We can learn to see differently and, in significant ways, culturally develop 'double vision'. In *Ku-ring-ai* Chase National Park north of Sydney where I spent many hours bushwalking with my husband, we too noted the different way of seeing the Milky Way displayed.[17] It is in the rock engravings, a legacy of the *Guringa/Kuringai* people who created them before smallpox arrived with the First Fleet and almost obliterated their people.[18]

Rod commented that, after thirty years of listening and working with peoples of Australian Indigenous descent, his opinion is that we can be truly enriched through their interpretation of the human experience.[19] Recipient of a Master of Science degree, he worked for many years as a science teacher at St Augustine's College, Brookvale (a suburb of Sydney) where, after the publication of *The Red Land* (his first book of poetry), he became part of the Red Land Club's initiatives. Rod devoted the rest of his life to creating a greater understanding of how Australian First Peoples can make a significant contribution to the religious thinking of the world. I have been most fortunate to be one of the people who met him in person, as well as through his artistic works born of deep reflection on the experience he gained.

The Red Land Club

In explaining the origins of The Red Land Club, Rod shared:

> One thing leads to another. An early edition of *The Red Land* book was published in 1972. Soon after that, a Red Land Club was formed at Saint Augustine's College in Brookvale, Sydney. Three boys started it as an entertainment club. It was not long before boys were writing their own music to some of the poems. On stage, they acted out Aboriginal stories with which they were familiar.
>
> At first, they were thinking mainly of entertaining relatives and friends at the college. But audiences grew and after a few years, the Red Land Club went on tour. Over the years they visited Perth, Adelaide, Cairns, Mareeba, Herberton, Innisfail, Cunnamulla, Charleville, Ulladulla, and Kyabram.
>
> In 1976 the Red Land Club performed at the Sydney Opera House. Like the wandering Spirit People of the Dreamtime, we still journey into the vast horizons of this Land.

For Rod, 'the Red Land' represented an Australia inclusive of the margins where the red soil is so vibrantly visible. The seeds of our collaboration began when I attended a concert by The Red Land Club in Perth.[20] At the time I had been assigned the literacy development of a group of students at the then Tardun Special Government Aboriginal School. I bought *The Red Land* book of Rod's poetry at the concert in the hope of gaining further inspiration for successfully doing my job – a task which the students themselves had told me in their own words was hopeless. I sought for expressions of commonalities expressed in English between their world and that of other Australians and Rod's work presented as a possible springboard. This search for commonalities and resonances seemed second nature to me as I had practised living and learning within a dominant 'Anglo' mainstream monoculture while living in a different European one in my home and extended family.

Of and In the Dust

Whenever he had experienced an extremely challenging day, one of my colleagues said he would turn his eyes to the ranges surrounding the community and remember the length of time they had been on this earth. Relativising difficult moments helped him sift the seeds of prioritisation against the backdrop of an enduring past. Here land became for him an image of immutable constancy.[21]

Someone has described Australia as 'a haunted land' and we can wonder about the, at times, frenzied headlong dash into the accumulation of material goods by some living here. This song celebrates our being in, and of the spirit, in and of this very land itself.

ANGELS IN THE DUST

We are angels in the dust
We are angels of the dust.

1. *The spirit of seeming long forgotten memories*
   Haunt us, taunt us.
   We are angels, angels, angels of the dust,
   Angels of the dust, angels of the dust.

2. *Consumer man*
   Wide-eyed in the market light
   Technology man
   Calling from the concrete canyon
   We are angels in the dust.

3. *Smothered with things*
   Drowning in a deluge of information
   We are angels, angels,
   Angels in the dust, angels in the dust

4. *We are truly human*
   And know that we are so
   Only when the wings of starlight
   Penetrate the dust
   And the Sacred embraces us,
   And the Sacred embraces us.
   We are angels, angels, angels in the dust
   We are angels, angels, angels of the dust.

   Lyrics: Rod Cameron, James Cornell
   Music: Maria Rosa

Red Land

At Innisfail in 1987, Rod introduced 'Red Land' thus: 'Maria has taken on the whole complex of ideas of "Red Land". The "Red Land" is Australia, a unique land, great though seemingly also cruel. It is a sacred land and all the ideas which come to our mind when we think of this great land of Australia, Maria has put into this song she has written. It is simply called "Red Land".' Here are its lyrics:

RED LAND

A red land sings in the sun,
A red land sings when the day is done.
She smiles every day at dawn,
She is forever born.

Her voice echoes where the eagles fly,
Grows silent where the river dies.
Her crevices hold tongues of fire,
Touching a strong, gentle heart's desire.

A red land sings in the sun,
A red land sings when the day is done.
She sings in stillness with heart on fire,
Ever deeper, ever higher.

> *Lyrics: Rod Cameron, Maria Rosa*
> *Music: Maria Rosa*

Rod and I held a series of concerts in 1987 showcasing the *Red Land Songs* at Mareeba, Cairns, Kuranda, Dimbulah and Innisfail. James Cornell accompanied us in all, dubbing himself 'the roadie'. This description aligns well with his pre-existent love and use of motorbikes! James had a deep love of the works of Gerard Manly Hopkins and significant experiences of living overseas immersed in other cultures. He and Rod developed a quick rapport through deep common interests and a shared sense of humour. Loretta Paolucci rendered invaluable assistance to this tour too.

When recording the *Red Land Songs*, Kerry Sanders played the flute. She is also one of the guitarists – others being Elizabeth

Giddey and myself – for this album. Yvonne Maulden wrote some of the harmony used and Sister Marie Langtry OSB helped with the production. All freely gave of our time and talent.

Rod read from *The Red Land* at the City Place Concert in Cairns on 26 January 1990, where he unveiled some of the *Red Land Songs* anew using recordings. According to sources, circa 500 people attended and watched the *Maubiag* dancers from the Torres Strait Islands perform too.

Fr Rod

CHAPTER 2

SINGING SILENCE

ALCHERINGA

Chorus:

Alcheringa. Alcheringa,
dreaming in the fire glow
calling to the stars of midnight.
Let the ancient rivers flow.
Let the ancient rivers flow.

1. *From deep darkness shines the light.*
   Morning brings a brighter day.
   Tell the stories through the night.
   Our songlines mark the sacred way.

Chorus

2. *The Dream is true. The Dream is real.*
   Behold the mystery of the land,
   the wonders that all things reveal,
   the deep voice of the silent sands.

Chorus

Lyrics: Rod Cameron
Music: Maria Rosa

On 12 December 1993, I received a small card pinned to a paper handwritten in Mareeba giving me the above lyrics. It read: 'Dear Maria, It would be good to have an Alcheringa song. Here are some words. What do you think? Rod.' I replied I would 'give it a go' and wrote the music. Here is some of the background to the song as articulated by Rod.

> There is a famous well-known anthropologist called Strehlow who, writing about 'The Dreamtime' stated that, in his opinion (he wrote this in a scientific report) the uniquely Australian contribution to the religious thinking of humanity is the Aboriginal conviction that eternity touches time. Now Strehlow is an anthropologist of first, highest rating and he is thoroughly scientific. He made that comment in a scientific context. It wasn't sort of just a pious thought that he flipped off his tongue. It was a serious statement that he made as an anthropologist. In his opinion, the uniquely Australian contribution to the religious thinking of mankind is the Aboriginal conviction of eternity touching time.
>
> Notice he did not say that this was a uniquely Australian contribution that was of interest to Aboriginal peoples. He didn't say it was just something of interest to Australians. He said this is a contribution to the religious thinking of all mankind – a uniquely Australian contribution. What on earth was Strehlow talking about? What is this that we call 'The Dreamtime'? The word 'Dreamtime' is a translation of the *Arrernte* word *Alcheringa* that means the 'eternal now'. We translate it – actually Spencer and Gillen translated the word in the 1880s. They used the word 'Dreamtime' and it has been used since. The word *Alcheringa* meaning 'eternal now' or 'eternity touching

time' is a view of the human condition. It is a view of the human condition for everybody, not just Aborigines. Aboriginal culture is not simply chasing goannas and swallowing witchetty grubs. The central thing is this *Alcheringa* or 'eternal now'.

Alcheringa is a view of the human condition and the view is this: that we humans live in time; that is our experience. We go from moment to moment, day to day. We see the passing of the seasons as the years roll on. We live in time. The moments pass by. That is the human experience. But to see the human experience only in time is not realistic. We experience some encounters with the sacred. The sacred is the human experience. We are in contact with it, we are aware of it, and we know that we are experiencing it. Some communication and presence of the sacred is in some way eternal – it is eternity.

Eternity is not conceived of in terms of time. Eternity is not a long time; eternity is not a long, long, long, long, long time. Eternity is no time. It is beyond time. It is beyond the dimensions of time and best conceived of in terms of life. There is some limitless life that is pouring down upon me and I am conscious of it. I am conscious of its presence and conscious of its influence. It is my consciousness of the sacred that affects every moment of my time. Eternity touches time in the human experience.

Now anyone who finds that to be their experience: that we live in time and eternity – horizontal time and eternity which is perpendicular – can be grounded in and open themselves limitlessly to the mysterious sacred that is the human condition. Anyone who in faith (and I do) accepts that this is the human condition, such a person is a person of the *Alcheringa*; such a person is a person of 'The Dreamtime', of the *Alcheringa* whether they are of Aboriginal descent or not. And that is what Strehlow meant when he said that this insight is a uniquely Australian contribution to the religious thinking of mankind.[1]

The anthropologist Rod is referring to above is Carl Friedrich Theodor Strehlow or his son Theodor Georg Heinrich Strehlow (Ted Strehlow) who linguistically studied the *Arrernte* in Central Australia. The Strehlow Research Centre in *Mparntwe*/Alice Springs honours their work. Rod, as was the custom then (and still is with some), used the term 'mankind' in the above commentary. Those who now focus on the power of more overtly inclusive language may use the term 'humankind' instead. Rod has, however, succinctly captured the essence of what many First Australians will now refrain from describing as 'The Dreamtime' – not because it is a 'wrong' translation but simply because many interpret the word 'dream' to mean something so distinct from this world of time that it omits the connection the sacred makes with time.

A group of Indigenous elders visited the tourism initiatives undertaken by First Nations people in Arnhem Land. They returned to their community with the firm conviction that they, in their tourism project, would not translate their corresponding word for *Alcheringa/Tjukurrpa/*other Indigenous language equivalents into the English 'Dreamtime'. They also spoke in English of what is *'true'* (a word captured in Rod's words for the song) to mean all-encompassing authenticity.

We cannot translate *Alcheringa/Tjukurrpa*/their correspondents directly and completely with an English word. 'Dreamtime' is a one-word translation that has emerged in English (as *Traumzeit* has in German) yet these terms are still inadequate for conveying all *Alcheringa/Tjukurrpa*/their correspondents in other Indigenous languages represent. The *Altyerre* in Eastern and Central *Arrernte* is 'the creation of the world and all things in it, and its eternal existence [often termed "the Dreaming" in English]'.[2] *Altyerrenge* (al-cher-eng-uh) with the emphasis on the second syllable means 'from the Altyerre times'.[3] *Altyerre, Arrernte* and *Altyerrenge* are written here in the international orthography used in the *Eastern and Central Arrernte to English Dictionary*.[4] From his sources, Rod used the word spelt as *Alcheringa,* and thus I have remained with his use of it. The 'true' in the lyrics is a description used by some Central Australian First Nations people to describe all that is connected to stories of ancestors' songs, a complex layering of all repositories of knowledge linked with meeting the sacred in time in the land of which we are part. As Rod has explained, we do not need to be an Aboriginal person to experience the sacred in time and that is partly why many Aboriginal people wish to appropriately share their world and understandings with others.

There are different layers of sharing and these are worked out in accompaniment with particular First Peoples. They are attentive to our capacity to absorb and can invite us into a form of attentiveness to which we are unaccustomed. This sharing can, among more traditionally oriented First Peoples, take a form of knowledge transmission in which we are not first presented with a full summary. We are led to parts of the knowledge slowly as we attend to physically walking through 'country'. The relevant story emerges with the unfolding 'country'.[5] Among many Australian First Nations people, we can only start to learn in 'country' via movement through it. An attentiveness to absorbing knowledge allows us to be educated in a different lifeworld if we focus on discovery rather than being argumentative, expectant of an academic dissertation, or acting like a quiz master. Thus, we permit ourselves to grow gracefully in more complete understanding.

'Songlines'

A co-worker who spoke the local Indigenous language fluently presented a diagram of the *Ascent of Mount Carmel* for me to one very remote community member with its explanation. He asked the local man what he thought of the ideas associated with this diagram. The man asked, 'Is this Christian?' My co-worker replied affirmatively. The local man said, 'Why have you not told us about this before? We know all about that!'[6]

My other source of lyrics, James Cornell, wrote: 'A group of Aboriginal people had just finished leading me through one of their stories in preparation for the tour program … It had been a powerful experience and had finished dramatically. I am sensitive to drama, and was reeling inwardly. But I wasn't given time to linger. The only person who had not spoken during the recounting of the story suddenly said, "And then a group of people appeared on that hill over there singing." And the song went on, and goes on continually, part of the Songlines that sing the country.'[7]

Mike Smith, in his article 'The Metaphysics of Songlines', describes Bruce Chatwin's reference to the term 'songlines' in 1987 as a 'bowdlerised version of Dreaming tracks (which) escaped into the public domain'.[8] He asserts: 'Songlines have many roles, but the popular ideas that they are mainly mnemonic maps, quasi-historical records, moral allegories or troves of ecological wisdom, are projections of contemporary concern. Aspects of these are implicit, or perhaps latent, in these narratives, but their primary role is as a kind of scripture, a framework for relating people to land, and to show this relationship is inalienable or "the law".[9]

He further claims Chatwin's use of the term 'songlines' propelled it into a form that 'replaced its religious trappings with metaphors'.[10] Smith also acknowledges a religious tradition not achieved anywhere else in the world.[11] Unfortunately, this tradition seems to have been caught up in the differences between pantheism and panentheism.[12]

Elements of the Eternal

Rod Cameron introduced the following song in 1987 as dealing with 'eternity streaming through the land. Maria wrote the words and the music for this and she uses the symbol of the stream flowing through this land.' His work inspired the content.

THE STREAM

There are often stories, stories we haven't heard.
They flow through the mountains and into the earth.
They live in the mountains and travel over plains,
In rivers and lakes and flooding rains.

Here's a story about this land,
A land that's ancient and new.
Here's a story about this land,
A land that welcomes you.

Through this land eternity flows like a stream,
It touches our desire to be free.

The land touches her people,
Is touching them still.
The land touches her people,
Is touching them still.

The land touches her people,
To her they belong.
The land touches her people,
Fills them with song, fills them with song.

Through this world eternity flows like a stream,
Calling all people to dignity.

> *Lyrics: Rod Cameron, Maria Rosa*
> *Music: Maria Rosa*

Meeting Presence Between Land and Mind

Not long after writing 'Black December', I attended a seminar/gathering called *The Land in Mind* hosted by the Australian and New Zealand Society of Jungian Analysts. It proved most informative and also provided a forum for relating to a series of 'land' dreams. Many years later while studying in the USA, I began having my own 'Australian' dreams. From them, I realised my psyche too connects with this land and its creatures – a land which James Cornell states our First Peoples 'mainline'.[13]

From his own experience, James asserts: 'The Aboriginal people have the love, the vision, the art, the stories, the spirituality to allow us to cross Australia's psychic mountain barrier, as they once could have led us past its physical imprisonment by the Blue Mountains.'[14] Earlier he had shared that, after a day spent with a historian in the

Blue Mountains, the man soberly said, 'The Aborigines had been walking across these mountains for centuries. If the white people had asked them, they would have been across decades earlier.'[15]

The following poem for which I composed music grew out of Rod's meeting between mind and land while on the Darling River in New South Wales.

ON THE DARLING
(Alternate Name: Red, Black and Gold)

The sky is a cathedral dome of blue,
A lofty eagle rides on rigid wings.
I rest the oars and I am gliding too,
Where no bush bird is heard, no locust sings.

With thirst from rowing in the ruthless sun,
I go ashore to boil some billy tea.
The red flames dance amid black crackling sticks,
Like ochred myalls in corroboree.

Through columned smoke there looms a river gum,
A giant of eucalypts with limbs like fire,
The flaking bark deep marked with red and gold,
As vested for some priesthood of desire.

The red flames dance amid black crackling sticks,
The flaking bark deep marked with red and gold,
Black, red and gold
Black, red and gold
Black, red and gold.

Lyrics: Rod Cameron
Music: Maria Rosa

Rod spoke of the experience at the Innisfail concert in 1987:

> Many of you would have met my brother Ralph Cameron. He is also a priest. He was up here in Innisfail a short while ago and he now teaches down at Villanova College in Brisbane. Prior to coming here in the north, I was teaching for thirty years myself so what you're looking at is an old worn-out, rundown science teacher! However, my brother Ralph is still labouring in the teaching field and, some years ago during the school holidays, we went to Bourke together. We hired a small motorboat. We went miles upriver and while there, the motor of the boat ceased to function. We went ashore to decide what was best to do. There, we met a farmer who offered to take us to Bourke. He allayed our fears of two people getting lost in the bush or being eaten by crocodiles!!!
>
> It was decided I would row the boat back to Bourke. I might mention in passing that Cairns is my hometown and there was a time when I was in the Cairns Rowing Club. Rowing back to Bourke was well within my capabilities. On the way there, I decided I would like to boil a cup of billy tea. I was so much younger then than I am now. I went over to the shore, got out the billy and some tea. I used to love doing that. I had a bit of lunch there on my own in the heart of Australia and, thinking about this afterward, I wrote this poem. In it, I mention the colour of the flames dancing amongst the black sticks and a column of smoke rising above the river campfire. A mighty red river gum had gold flaking on its bark. The gold, in particular, inspired me to write this little poem called 'On the Darling'.

Maria sings this and other poems and her music puts a new dimension into them, sort of releases them. She expands them, making them more beautiful than I thought they were myself. That is what she's done with this poem. She saw in these red flames, black crackling sticks, column smoke, golden flake of the bark, the colours of the red, black and gold now part of the Aboriginal flag. The black represents the First Peoples and the red is the land. Red is a sacred colour and the gold in the centre is the spirit uniting and permeating the people and the land. Uniting the spirit of the land with the people and animals, all are one in the spirit of red, black and gold. If you read the poem (in my book *The Red Land*), you'll see what Maria has done with it in the song 'Red, Black and Gold'.

The Aboriginal flag is now one of the three official flags of Australia under *The Flags Act 1953*. Via now ubiquitous exposure, the visible presence of this flag helps counter the existence of a 'psychological *terra nullius*' – the remains of the fiction of *terra nullius* in historical memories, institutional and behavioural patterns of many other Australians. In addressing the consequences of psychological *terra nullius*, Larissa Behrendt, Professor of Law and Indigenous Studies at the University of Technology, Sydney, asserts that Prime Minister John Howard's rhetoric 'brushed over the historical context in which dispossession took place. Howard used the rhetoric of equal laws for all Australians to justify his political stance claiming there should be no special laws for one section of the Australian public.'[16] This begs the question: What is the difference between equality and equity?

Unfortunately, the rhetoric of equal laws for all Australians did not extend to cover the suspension of the *Commonwealth 1975 Racial Discrimination Act* (RDA) which the Howard government enacted to ensure 'The Intervention' could legally go ahead. Subsequently, for equality's sake, it needed reinstatement.[17] Via suspension of the RDA, members of communities affected by the legislation associated with 'The Intervention' effectively were 'denied the protections afforded by the RDA to every other citizen to challenge the legislation that they consider in breach of the RDA'.[18] Arguing 'special measures' as a necessary part of the 'emergency response' to child sexual abuse in the NT, this Federal Government's one-size-fits-all approach swept up innocent people and targeted them in the same way as possible offenders. Such an approach has not been enacted elsewhere in mainstream responses to institutional child sexual abuse even where sexual abuse has been proven in many cases. Nuance existed for the latter but it did not in seventy-three prescribed NT communities. In disbelief and shock I, like many, naively had assumed the RDA could not be suspended and land management could not be affected the way it was via its suspension.

Land rights as an issue became clearer to me when I first taught in the NT. The 1976 *Aboriginal Land Rights Act (Northern Territory)* passed in December of that year proved groundbreaking as it permitted First Peoples to claim land where traditional ownership could be proven.[19] I realised that where a claim proved successful some of the crippling dynamics associated with colonisation had been given a very real chance of being changed. After a long fight, the *Pitjantjatjara Land Rights Act* came into effect in South Australia too. It is now formerly known as the *Anangu Pitjantjara Yankunytjatjara Land Rights Act 1981*.

Circa another Easter, I attended a significant meeting in Wilcannia. I remember travelling to this beautiful part of New South Wales drinking in the scenery from a converted milk truck. One evening, a film in black and white concerning the NT massacre at Coniston was featured at the gathering. This broadened my ever-deepening awareness and understanding of much veiled in a shroud of silence over the years. Although I had previously met Janine Roberts while volunteering for a Melbourne organisation concerned with Aboriginal rights and read her book *From Massacres to Mining*, the film strongly impacted me. Thankfully, as part of truth-telling and an innate impetus towards healing, veils around this country's history are still slowly being lifted. My interest in how the intentional or unintentional impacted the lives of my young Indigenous students grew. The substance of the 2017 *Uluru Statement from the Heart* has since underlined the importance of ongoing attention and informed engagement by all citizens in understanding what will assist in transforming current contexts.

The following song celebrates our learning to live together peacefully – not simply multiculturally side by side but interculturally: enriched by two-way deep knowledge exchange and understanding of each other. Thus, one in heart, we can be free from the limited understandings which crucify those who operate differently from the mainstream dominant culture. This song celebrates the land now called Australia as well as its diverse peoples. I decided to write this song as, at one school where I taught, my colleagues and I met students from ninety-two nationalities with various religious backgrounds! People of First Nations heritage also marry those with overseas heritage. We can celebrate these unions alongside relationships which work for the benefit of all.

Our First Nations too are not uniform. Their concept of 'country' means life-oriented stories can be held by all. Let us reach out in spirit from the sacred within place, our inner selves, and grow stronger via embracing diversity beyond tokenism.

AUSTRALIA

Australia, our country,
May we shine in unity.
Though from many origins,
One in heart to be.

Australia, our country,
May we shine in diversity.
Though from many origins,
One in heart to be.

Looking deep to her soul,
We see red, black and gold,
She holds us in her hand.
So, on mountains steep,
In valleys deep,
In faith in her we sleep.

Australia, our country,
May we pray for unity.
Though from many origins,
One in freedom to be.
One in freedom to be.

Lyrics: Rod Cameron, Maria Rosa
Music: Maria Rosa

Anchoring Diversity

How we can leverage diversity is something requiring our ongoing honest attention. We can begin by asking ourselves questions like: How do we foster the expression of purposeful leadership by people of Australian Indigenous descent? Do we create space for their agency? Do we ask them what resources they need rather than presuming we know? How long will we accept male dominance by those of non-Indigenous descent where it operates rather than developing complementarity in partnership? How do we continually normalise dominance in the exercise of power?

Crystal M Fleming sagely makes the following point:

> Learning about any axis of oppression (much less multiple axes of oppression!) can feel overwhelming and daunting, to say the least. That's why it's so important to recognise that you cannot take on all the troubles of the world. No-one can wave a magic wand and make human suffering disappear – and we're only on this planet for an infinitesimally short moment of time. When students ask me for direction, I try to convey the importance of choosing an area of impact that bridges their interests with their unique talents. But, to do this, you have to invest some time and energy in self-exploration. No-one can tell you what your purpose is (that's your job), but if you are having a hard time narrowing down your talents, you might ask friends, family members and mentors to help you identify your gifts and strengths.[20]

My gifts and strengths have been useful and helpful in various contexts in which 21% of Australia's Indigenous populations live: remote areas.[21] These hold communities which can be strongly marginalised and structurally misunderstood – ones in which their gifts and strengths are not structurally valued or supported. Mark Moran asserts, 'The intractability of Indigenous disadvantage in Australia is undeniable.'[22] Even amidst intense public debate about underlying causes and possible solutions, 'Indigenous disadvantage in Australia has also proven to be higher and more intractable than that experienced by their Indigenous counterparts in Canada, New Zealand and the United States.'[23]

Mark Moran summarises one perspective on the Federal Government Intervention whose aftermath I witnessed and experienced:

> Public opinion and media are potent drivers of Indigenous affairs policy. There was a string of shocking media reports of child neglect and abuse in remote Indigenous communities through 2006 and 2007. The Howard Government's response was to launch the Northern Territory Emergency Response … in the lead-up to the 2007 Federal election. At a time when his government was trailing in the polls, was a legitimate concern for citizen welfare weighed against the political gains of 'sending in the troops'? Academic economist Boyd Hunter questioned the timing – as the reports of child abuse had long been known – and the military framing of the response. He also questioned why the Intervention was limited to the Northern Territory, as the then known cases of child abuse and neglect among Indigenous children were lower compared to other jurisdictions.[24]

Later, the Royal Commission into Institutional Responses to Child Sexual Abuse held between 13 January 2013 and 15 December 2017 gives us an insight into similar cases and subsequent responses in other jurisdictions involving non-Indigenous children and perpetrators. The latter did not mirror the multipronged extent of the response in the NT's seventy-three prescribed remote communities in 2007. This raises many uncomfortable questions.

Because remote 'Indigenous communities are marginalised both socially and geographically, governments face many cultural and logistical challenges in delivering services to them.'[25] 'Policy powerfully determines what happens on the ground in remote Aboriginal communities, often in unintended and surprising ways. No matter how well a policy is conceived, delivery on the ground is where it counts, and where it consistently fails. It helps to understand that many of the drivers of Indigenous affairs policy do not derive from the place where it is intended to serve. Some do, but many do not. And the opinions that the public hold matter more than they think.'[26]

One person who has immersed herself in the practice of localised life-enhancing interculturation is Deborah Ruiz Wall who, though born in the Philippines, has lived most of her life in Australia. The Australian Commonwealth Government in 2004 awarded her an Order of Australia medal for her service to the community in the areas of social justice, reconciliation and multiculturalism. She has been a member of the Women's Reconciliation Network which produced *Around the Kitchen Table* – a work on reconciliation by women from diverse ethnic and religious backgrounds from Aboriginal and Torres Strait Islander, English, Irish, Filipino, Greek, Jewish and Muslim communities.[27] Born into an ethnically diverse family, one of Deborah's assertions with which I partly resonate is: 'Biculturalism is my identity.'[28]

Depending on the depth of one's immersive experiences, hybrid identities are possible. We hear of hybrid vehicles which, depending on contextual needs, may be switched between running on electricity or some other energy source. Immersed in other cultures, human beings can code-switch to achieve a greater sense of cultural safety and the best possible outcomes in exchanges. Indeed in 1993, pondering fluidity and many-sidedness, Robert J Lifton wrote of the protean self. Perhaps it is what makes deep intercultural living possible despite its enormous challenges.

A Kimberley boab

CHAPTER 3

CIRCA KING SOUND

BOABAB TREE
*(Alternative name: **TREE SPIRIT**)*

The black man in chains
A prisoner was he
Within the hollow trunk.
Alone within the heart
Of a bo-o-o-ab tree.

He sang his living song,
He sang it tenderly,
And eagles came to rest
On the branches of the boab tree
To listen and to rest.

They could not see the man,
A vanished tribe was he,
But still they hear his song
In the boab tree
His mighty spirit song
His mighty spirit song.

Lyrics: Rod Cameron
Music: Maria Rosa

In responding to evidence of Australia's sometimes unacknowledged sad history, Rod Cameron pointed out:

> Near Derby in the Kimberley region, just outside the town, there is a big tree, a boab tree that has a very wide trunk. The trunk is hollow. It is called 'The Prison Tree'. There's also one up near Wyndham. Ten, fifteen, or even twenty people can squeeze in there, it's so big in the hollow inside. It's not a very high tree, has a huge bulbous trunk and looks like a big Christmas pudding sitting out in a landscape. There are a few straggly branches coming out of the top of it. It is called 'The Christmas Tree' by some. Occasionally some Aboriginal people who had been arrested for some reason or other were brought to Wyndham or Derby. They would be chained and spend the night in this substitute lock-up. That's why the one in Derby is called 'The Prison Tree'. Tourist buses go past it now and the bus driver tells the tourists the story. It's a really sad story and I wrote this little poem about it called 'Tree Spirit'.[1]

It seems that at one point the words 'Hillgrove Lockup' marked the Wyndham Boab (*Adansonia gregorii*) Prison Tree which served as a halfway and overnight stop between Old Halls Creek and Old Wyndham. From this holding place on the King River Road, prisoners ended up in Perth, Rottnest and other jails.[2] The veracity of the stories of actual incarceration inside 'The Prison Tree' in the 1890s in Derby has been challenged by researchers Dr Elizabeth Grant of the University of Adelaide and University of Tasmania's Dr Kristin Harman. The manager of the Derby Visitor Centre, Ms Jenny Kloss, states chaining of prisoners to trees occurred around it instead.[3] It is on occasion difficult to distinguish oral tradition from grapevine effects in the telling of stories. Dr Grant shares that we know Aboriginal people used boab trees to store dead bones and hopes those found in the Derby Prison Tree will one day be located. *Jandamarra*, a resistance fighter from the *Bunuba* people spent some time in Derby in jail.[4]

Some First Nations people when I lived in Derby spoke *Nyikina* and some of their turbulent contact history has been documented. People of Malay and Filipino heritage also married into some First Nations families there. When invited to meet me as their children's new teacher over damper and tea at the school, I felt joyously overwhelmed by the welcoming engagement of kin and their expressed care for their children.

Bungarun Leprosarium

Attempting to learn *Nyikina* as my first Indigenous language sparked in me what has become over the years a strong interest in these languages. To augment my teacher training, I enrolled in a couple of Linguistics subjects offered by the now Edith Cowan University. The existence of the functioning Derby leprosarium became for me a symbol of the existence of deeper knowledge outside my experience. The leprosarium stood on the outskirts of the town of Derby. One day I visited it.

A high wire fence surrounded the leprosarium to protect those receiving treatment from the roaming marshland crocodiles as well as, initially, preventing people from leaving. I imagined a crocodile or two snapping on the other side of the high wire fence when the tide rose as it did so powerfully in this and other parts of King Sound. I have since learned that only in the later years of the 1940s had effective microbials emerged to combat the mildly infectious cause of leprosy – the microorganism *Mycobacterium leprae* and, then much later, *Mycobacterium lepromatosis* (discovered in 2008).[5] Established in 1936, the St John of God Sisters staffed the leprosarium called *Bungarun* as part of the standard isolation treatment then demanded for those afflicted. Paucibacillary (PB) leprosy is less infectious and aggressive than Multibacillary leprosy (MB) yet the right course of multidrug therapy can still cure someone with MB.

As a young adult from Gippsland, Victoria, realising the existence of leprosy in Derby both surprised and startled me. In my mind, it was a disease belonging principally to Biblical times. After reading the text *Who Walk Alone* by Perry Burgess for English Literature at Teachers' College, I somehow assumed it only existed in other countries.[6] I am puzzled now as to why I assumed this to be true. The main character of *Who Walk Alone* – a war veteran – only discovered he had the disease after being home for many years. This attested to the long incubation period of Hansen's Disease (HD), an alternate name for leprosy. The soldier had been exposed to the bacteria when he fought overseas. The prospect of his family having to deal with his development of HD stirred this American war veteran to fake his death. Then he moved to The Sanctuary of Sorrow in Manila in the Philippines where he could be with other sufferers and receive the care available to all there.

Those from Australian First Nations who had HD introduced via European settlement found themselves detained for treatment. Reluctant to volunteer for the necessary isolation from 'country' and family constituting the core strategy in HD's then early management, authorities forcibly relocated them. Before 1936, authorities transported all diagnosed with leprosy in the Kimberley by boat to Darwin, some in heavy neck chains because they did not wish to go.[7] Many feared they would never return home or see loved ones again as seemed to happen to many they knew who fell into the sphere of Western medicine. After caring for 1200 detainees for over 50 years, the leprosarium closed on 5 September 1986. Government health services then managed the disease via alternative means. I have since learned that 350 people died and now lie in *Bungarun's* cemetery, each grave marked by a white cross. A large wall lists the name of all deceased. When I visited, the leprosarium still operated as a full-time care facility.[8]

My students in Derby spoke English in a way unfamiliar to me. I thus became aware of Aboriginal English with its differing associated areas of meaning for Standard English words such as 'shame', 'deadly' and 'flash'. The language Kriol became the subject of one of my study assignments: a contrastive analysis between it and English. Thus, it became clear to me how unsafe it is to make assumptions because something looks or sounds familiar, such as the statement *Im* (pronounced eem) *breakim im arm* which described the actual severing of part of an arm from the rest of the body. Also, a child in the playground could bully another differently – the complaint *I* (pronounced ee) *bin call my fa* referred to a taunt received which referenced one's father. I learned to avoid concluding that what I heard was simply broken English without word patterns, structures, other meanings and associations.

The statement *I* (pronounced ee) *bin makim a miss-take* described not exactly hitting the mark, like for example, throwing a goal in basketball and missing the basket. I liked this expression as it emphasised 'missing' a desired goal or target rather than a person being defective. As growing human beings, we cannot always perform perfectly. Sometimes we even miss the point of what someone is saying. We *miss*-understand why further unprejudiced attention is warranted. Part of the above statement's elegance for me lay in its correct portrayal in Aboriginal English of an element of learning: getting it wrong the first, second, third and, goodness knows how many other times, only indicated more practice is needed. Via the use of this statement in the classroom, students neatly named this truth to each other without blame or derision and enabled making another attempt without fear of being mocked.

Wandjina

Amid the diversity characterising the First Nations people in what is designated as the Kimberley region by mainstream Australians, their belief systems have confronted those of various missionaries. Sifting to find a balance between these belief systems is a task some take on more publicly than others. During 2021, the NAIDOC (National Aborigines and Islanders Day Observance Committee) week, an ABC (Australian Broadcasting Corporation) program focused on the NAIDOC theme 'Heal Country'. The program featured some people in the Kimberley. In it, Pastor Kirsty *Burgu* pointed out God lives outside the church – 'The church is just a building.'[9]

Janet *Oobagooma*, *Worrorra* elder at Mowanjum, outside Derby in the west Kimberley, informs the viewer 'God is a Wandjina.'[10] We learn 'The Worrorra, Ngarinyin and Wunambal people believe the Wandjina created the land, the sea and the law for people to live by. They are deeply spiritual and sacred figures, central to the belief system of the oldest continually living culture on earth.'[11] Commenting on a previously experienced sense of displacement, Pastor Kirsty *Burgu* asserts: 'Without my culture, like knowing where I come from, where my ancestors came from, what their stories were, I wasn't really a whole person.'[12] Ron Bopf OSA composed the music for the following lyrics of his confrère Rod Cameron. It is mindful of the place of the *Wandjina* in the ongoing creation and local cultural understanding. I particularly love the line: *'Shuffling skirts of stirring leaves'*. This song also reminds me of the practice of singing out to the spirits when one enters new country with a First Nations person.

WANDJINA

The moon is lonely by the sea,
Lonely night birds in the tree,
Softly tones their doleful plea,
Come Wandjina. Come!

Silver ripples on the lake,
Criss-cross circles they make.
Moonglow lilies are awake,
Come Wandjina. Come!

Gently moves the spirit breeze,
Shuffling skirts of stirring leaves,
Whispering secrets to the trees,
Come Wandjina. Come!

Come Wandjina, Wandjina come.
Come Wandjina, come.
Come Wandjina, Wandjina come.
Come Wandjina, come.

Lyrics: Rod Cameron
Music: Ron Bopf

Learning to speak *Worrorra* and using it to translate the gospel of Mark, the Presbyterian missionary Rev James Robert Love opened himself 'enough to look for images of God, the reflection of God' within the local culture.[13] He visited *Wandjina* caves, listened to traditional stories and, talking with people about them, concluded: 'Well, look, God's been there, right there in your beginning. Your Lailai, your Dreamtime.'[14]

Desert brumbies

CHAPTER 4

WELCOMING PRESENCE

LA GRANGE
(Alternate name: Dreamtime Music)

At La Grange on the beach,
Where deserts end, last horizons reach,
Twilight people built a fire,
Whispered their hearts' desire.

Chants of old ever new,
Settled as gently as the dew,
Called to the land whose soft reply,
Sent sound of music to the sky.

Open your heart to the sound of music,
Echoing faintly in the stream,
As far away as in your dreams.

Chorus:

Dreamtime music haunts my heart,
Reminds me I can always start,
To touch the eternal with our dream
Dance to the music of the stream,
O dance to the music of the stream.

On legs black as ebony,
She ran across the sands to me,
Into my arms she sprang,
Then the heavens rang.

Her laughter sent music to the sky,
The moon played magic with her eyes,
She laughed in boundless ecstasy,
Deep joys of victory.

Chorus

> *Lyrics: Rod Cameron, Maria Rosa*
> *Music: Maria Rosa*

Rod shared the following at the Innisfail concert in 1987:

> I don't go boiling the billy much now. I can't get up without assistance! If I go down, I need help to get up again! The next song is called 'Dreamtime Music'. I won't read the poem on which it is based because it's a very long one. The song is the longest that Maria has written till now. As far as the experience involved, it is probably the most important one. In 1960, I was at

a place called La Grange on the coast miles south of Broome. I was sitting on a beach there and behind me were hundreds of miles of desert land, arid land, sacred desert, the Sandy and Gibson Deserts going all the way to the *Uluru*/Ayers Rock area. Before me was the vast coast of the Indian Ocean in the decline of the day. I was watching the sun set into the ocean – an unfamiliar sight for us from north Queensland.

Here I was between the great depths of the sacred desert and the depths of the sea, on this river of sand and, about twenty yards from me, was a group of Aborigines of the *Karajarri* people. Hardly any of those present could speak any English at all and, once again, I became extremely conscious of being a stranger in this land, a lonely man.

There was a little fire we had built on the beach and the dimming light of the sunset. A canopy of stars looked down on this lonely little spark of light within the vast mystery of the world. I had the feeling or the intuition that this was a sacred land to me too. I became conscious of the fact that this man was in a special time and the end of that day was something special. Next, a very simple thing happened … very often simple things are the most profound of all. A little girl of about nine or ten, one from the Aboriginal group of the *Karajarri* just leapt up, ran across the sand, past the fire, and threw herself into my arms. She was laughing. She laughed. That's all that happened.

As I held that little laughing child in my arms, I could hardly hold the tears from my eyes. I knew that this for me was a sacred moment. From that moment, I realised

Aborigines play an important part in the Australian experience of the Sacred. I have felt an empathy for them. I have never studied anthropology at university and I have never taken or made an academic study of Aboriginal cultures or Aboriginal languages but mine was a spiritual experience of great depth and it related me not only to these Aborigines but to this land, to this universe. And from that moment I felt more deeply Australian than I had ever felt before and I have never again felt a stranger in this land.

I belong to this land, I am of this land and in my encounters with its Aboriginal people since, I have sensed them being aware of that. They have told me many of their secrets. Now Maria Rosa has taken this already sacred event, this simple but sacred event, and seen the universal significance of it. She speaks of Dreamtime music as though she senses that there is music in the silence of that night and she has given this dimension to the song 'Dreamtime Music'. Maria has understood the very deepest meaning of that sacred event.

The incident to which Rod refers is later described in a newspaper article as 'a welcome that bridged thousands of years of separation. Since that simple, striking acceptance from an Aboriginal child Fr Rod has kept a strong empathy with the Aboriginal people.'[1] My own experience of *Bidyadanga*/La Grange resonated with Rod's and it is why I chose to write music for his poem about it. I remember fondly trips to nearby beaches, the ever-changing tides, the joy of children when they realised the old blue F100 pointed its nose towards the beach and they could get a lift there. One day we all had the most glorious mud bath thanks to the tide. Seagulls at times seem to fill the air. We also came across a death adder in the dunes and gave it a wide berth. In one location I found the most exquisitely beautiful cowrie shell.

Women in the community carried buckets filled with flour for damper-making on their heads (a photo of women similarly carrying firewood is shown in *Every hill got a story*).[2] They also would carry their shopping in a box this way and even a stack of four large bread loaves from the bakery. For the frail older people, a Mini Moke acted as a taxi service. The tides brought fish into the fish traps; fish thus gathered were taken back to the community to be eaten especially by those in mourning. At that time, those in particular relationships with the deceased customarily ate fish for a set amount of time rather than other kinds of meat.

The community had an interest in cattle and one day I found myself being asked to count the animals as they filed into the stockyards. Having spent my teenage years on a farm with cattle, I did this by counting the rumps passing the gate post furthest from where I stood. When the stockman swung off his horse, I announced the number (quite large) so he could pass it on to the guy in charge of the records. He smiled and said, 'Yes, that's right. The red one with a white blaze down its forehead and the dark one with the extra floppy ears are missing.' Astounded, I realised he had used a different way of working out the number of stock present. He knew the herd intimately so could report any absences just as I could – without counting – when someone did not show up for my class. By counting, I knew the number of cattle present but he knew which particular members of the herd had avoided muster. An example of holding 'haecceity'?

In another community, the school liaison officer smilingly spoke of 'mustering the kids' when he did his daily round reminding them the time to start walking to school had come. I loved the connection with horses that many communities and their members had. On our Gippsland farm, our horse Creamy ended up mostly ridden by my sister. However, I rode Jock as often as I could to the local river along a bush track. A magnificent 16.2 hand reddish sorrel thoroughbred, I would let him set the pace once we turned for home. Being on his back then truly felt like flying. One of my community co-workers, Teresa, also had a passion for horses and I dedicated this song to her. It is also a tribute to the horsemanship of First Peoples which assisted many stations to function successfully over many years alongside a celebration of the life of the senses.

RIDING INTO THE WIND – FOR TERESA

I gallop along where the bush gums sway
I gallop along with the wind
I gallop through the heat of the day
I gallop along with the wind.

Smell the air as it smooths your face
Feel the sun get in your skin
Away, away, the clouds race
And your joy is swelling in.

Through the bubbling river we go
Up the bank, up, up high
Wow, look at the dust go
As the cattle hit the dry.

I love the beautiful clear blue skies
I love the breeze that roams so free
I pray that everyone tries
And will be able to be.

WELCOMING PRESENCE

I ride along where the bush birds fly
I ride into the wind
I see green and browns flash by
I ride into the wind
I ride into the wind.

Lyrics and Music: Maria Rosa

High brumby numbers became a topic of conversation in one community and an item of the land management agenda concerning the fragile desert environments. Young men worked hard and had great fun rounding up the brumbies. With brumbies in the stockyards, a call would be put through to a trucking company so they could send a vehicle for their transportation the next day. On more than one occasion, however, someone would open the gates during the night and set the brumbies free. Then an early morning call had to hastily be made to cancel the truck!!! Inquiries yielded the intel that the brumbies are family members – kin – and people could not bear the thought of their relatives being sent away! Another approach thus had to be employed to manage brumby numbers.

Station life proved to be the norm for many First Peoples. The 75th anniversary of the Pilbara Strike organised by Law men Dooley Bin Bin and Clancy McKenna with unionist Don McLeod was celebrated on 1 May 2021. The strike for better working conditions and a minimum wage lasted for three years. It proved to be a masterful organisation of many First Nations people working on stations. Searching for information back then regarding these times, I acquired a copy of *Jigalong Mob: Aboriginal Victors Desert Crusade* by Robert Tonkinson.[3]

Once, people from out Jigalong way visited the community in which I lived. Tension filled the air. During the night, someone tapped on our accommodation door. On opening it, we ladies (who slept in what was affectionately called 'The Big House' where all staff meals were served) discovered a lass who said she did not wish to go away with the visitors and asked if we could hide her. Frightened and unsure, we said she could shelter for the night. When asked to drive young women further south, one of the lay missionaries refused, saying some did not wish to go and he did not want to be part of forcing them. Delicate intercultural diplomacy proved necessary, a task at which the linguist resident priest excelled. As in some other contexts, 'marriage' or being 'promised' became an issue of concern initiated by the women involved. Sons and daughters running away and partnering with someone from the wrong 'skin' group – a 'poison' cousin – also proved a source of deep angst for parents and other relatives if it occurred. Even though community members invariably welcomed them back if they returned, those involved had to ultimately 'face the music' of their transgressions according to First Law.

Interpathy

My Tardun students had informed me when I introduced myself: 'You will get nowhere with us Miss Maria.' 'Why?' I asked. 'We have dog's brains,' they replied. I queried: 'Who told you that?' and they answered, 'The people at the station.' 'Well,' I said, 'I have news for you. They are wrong.' Then I questioned them about what they liked doing. 'Making up songs' proved to be their first preference. So, we made a deal: we would compose songs together, write the words on the blackboard (so I would not forget them!), and use these words to learn how to write other ones. The first song they shared with me took the form of an apology, begging pardon of the station owners for the chickens which had broken into the homestead garden. It revealed 'interpathy' on their part, a term I will explain further. In this initial exchange, I realised what unnecessary hurdles the internalisation of negativity had created in these senior primary youngsters. The first song they wrote featured their language as well as English.

Finding ourselves as bystanders or being pulled into some delicate situations simply via our presence, it is important to consciously orient ourselves to develop 'interpathy' or empathy cognisant and inclusive of cultural understandings and frameworks being placed *vis-a-vis* each other. Labelling something unfamiliar as 'the work of the devil' as some do is unhelpful. René Girard has written extensively about this kind of labelling in human dynamics. In this field of intercultural challenge, such descriptions can regrettably sweep up and be applied to any form of assertion by First Nations elders, such as closing a road while people involved in ceremonies cross it. Judging such activity as 'the work of the devil' undermines elders' authority, particularly with the young. Taking a step back however for reflection, we can allow ourselves to see parallels in our society, such as the closing of a road for funerals and other processions, protests, declaration of emergency in situations of dangerous conditions such as bushfires and a global pandemic. Because a way of behaving does not mirror how we would act or expect in a particular moment in time does not automatically make it 'the work of the devil'. Unfortunately, such judgements can still be loudly promulgated by some Christians. Making accusations can become a habit, almost a sport of preference when operating differences are ignored and their observance is not graced with a flexible mindset.

A presentation by Johann Cilliers in 2007 introduced me to the word 'interpathy' which encapsulates the approach that the exercise of respect ultimately demands. He explains 'interpathy' contributes to the possibility of intending to create 'a spiritual space of intimacy, where reciprocal enrichment can take place' in South Africa, where society – like that in Australia – 'is indeed a multi-layered phenomenon, with different levels of possible analysis, perspectives and meanings'.[4] Interpathy allows the balm of respectful kindness to heal and newness to grow. It helps create safe spaces in which we can explore solutions, and grow together as human beings on a journey facing the demands and vicissitudes of life. A *malpa* or equivalent can even be assigned to assist your growing understanding of how best to proceed as a member of a minority in a community of predominantly First Nations people.[5] Alternatively, finding someone willing to act as a 'cultural broker' also makes being constructively present so much easier.

Practising interpathy does not automatically mean we have 'gone native' or romanticise other ways of being. It involves staying true to who we are, to our non-negotiables, and allowing others to have their similar parameters contoured by their current understandings and ours. Exercising coercive control via the power of one's position as a member of the majority is itself an abuse. That is why uninformed culturally biased 'fire and brimstone' attacks on others' long-term ways of being from pulpits do not work. Unless cowered into submission, people will simply stop going to church. Fostering dialogue and allowing ourselves to be educated by people within the innate dynamism of different non-static cultures are more productive approaches. We do not need to become carbon copies of each other to be of life-affirming assistance.

After sitting through one particular tirade at a church service, one First Nations teenager asked me as we sat down to breakfast whether she could say 'Grace'. She said she wished to pray for the sermoniser as she 'felt sorry for him'. Her response to the situation expressed compassion in Aboriginal English and, in this case, interpathy. I thought it a most kind gesture after what we had just sat through. Caught in a similar whirligig, a newly arrived student had been instructed to 'Throw this into the incinerator' when he was handed a large plastic bin. I found him later standing outside the administrator's office and checked if all was okay. He said he was in trouble because he threw the bin into the incinerator as asked!

Not taking any responsibility for the choice of words or sentence construction, the administrator only saw insubordination rather than misunderstanding and sent the young man home – some hours distance by plane! Years later, visiting the community from which the young man had come, I heard someone call out: 'Miss Maria!' I turned and saw a strikingly tall man who said, 'Do you remember me?' 'Of course,' I said. 'The bin!' and we both laughed. What else could we do? I tried to understand the perspective of the administrator at the time yet found his actions unnecessarily harsh. Had he employed interpathy or been open to dialogue about English being at risk of being literalised when it is not the first language, a different outcome would have been possible for the newcomer. It is hard to watch some events unfold and realise alternate viewpoints or explanations can be so summarily dismissed. Exercising interpathy can help customise our responses and grow in understanding a situation better via creating a follow-up space in which dialogue can materialise. When I asked a New York railway attendant for further instructions, she replied: 'Explain what you have understood please. If the signage does not work by itself, I need to know.' Rather than assuming we always get it completely right, searching for explanations facilitates greater clarity.

Listening – Though Sometimes 'Liar but!'

It is important to note not all station life was the same. We may, in Tinglish, jokingly say 'Same, same but different' for various people's experiences.[6] Alice Duncan-Kemp's writings reveal genuine efforts occurred in relationships across the cultural divides on her parents' cattle station called *Mooraberrie*.[7] Ladies I met at *Kundat Djaru*/Ringers Soak excitedly showed me around what remained of where they grew up on Gordon Downs station. No bad memories surfaced in the telling of stories that day. On the way there, we came to what looked to me like a sizeable river crossing. The passengers guided me into the middle of the water and then directed me to turn right!!! I asked, 'Won't we get bogged?!?' 'No, no,' they said, 'It is all stones in the middle.' Listening to them because I did not know the way, I drove the 'Troopie' a considerable way upriver without it missing a beat and, at one spot they again said, 'Turn right here!'[8] We then smoothly exited the beautiful clear water with an amazingly clean vehicle! That day I relearnt the value of trusting the locals who know the country – and the value of keeping moving!

The name *Kundat Djaru* means 'together-as-one'. The Community is also called *Yaruman* and the *Tjurabalan* people (who speak *Walmatjarri* and *Jaru*) gained legal recognition of their native title rights to this land on 20 August 2001.[9] When I visited post-2010, the country had received ample rain, and wildflowers prolifically covered it. It shone in all its wondrous splendour. The name of the largest watercourse near *Kundat Djaru* is Sturt Creek. That name, regrettably, is associated with a grim massacre that occurred circa 1922.[10]

I turn now to stories of Lenore Wilson who married Walter Camp in 1958 and lived on Floraville Downs – a station in Queensland's Gulf country. Rod gave me a photo of part of this property which Walter bought in 1963. It is 'very close to the Leichardt and Alexandra Falls – a spectacular sight to see when in flood'.[11] Walter built a cross there which powerfully asserted 'God Is.'

Lenore shared a couple of hilarious anecdotes of her experience associated with language difference and where they had previously lived: 'I went into Burketown one time and caught up with some of our Aboriginal women who came in from Calvert with us. They were in high spirits and very excited to tell me: "Mrs Camp, we been doing really well. You know there is people in town wanting to pay us 10 cents for every tribal word we can tell them. We been having fun making up word and getting paid".'[12]

When I first went to Derby, students staying at the hostel would often tell me something slightly dramatic or outlandish. Upon my responding with 'Really, wow! How about that!' they would reply with a delightful 'Liar but!' often accompanied by a little skip indicating they too had taken me 'for a ride'. They enjoyed telling 'tall tales' immensely and a humorous, light-hearted game developed.

Lenore also recalled that: 'When she went into town to have her third child – a son, Ernie – her two daughters were taken to a childcare centre for the day. The effect of the native language on the two children became evident when Lenore received a frantic call from the childcare centre, asking what nationality she was. Her daughters would not speak English and were talking to each other in a strange tongue, which turned out to be the native language of the Indigenous people they had grown up with – Garawa.'[13]

Going Native!

Any acknowledgement of strengths displayed by First Nations people by a non-Indigenous person could attract the accusation you had 'gone native' – truly (it is implied) a most undesirable state of affairs! No wonder many First Australian children's self-esteem seemed to hit depressingly shame-filled depths. Upon one of my fellow workers commenting on the obvious beauty of one young First Nations woman, a superintendent simply replied, 'You have been here too long!'

Happily, Rod's work countered such dampening of graced eyes and spirits and, in the song below, his life-enhancing perception is celebrated. I wrote it at his request for an event in Cairns at which students from Mount Saint Bernard, Herberton sang their rendition. It links in with *'the little laughing girl'* who, jumping into Rod's arms had, in boundless ecstasy, laughed *'Deep joys of victory'*.

WHEN THE WATTLES BLOOM

1. *Dark children now are coming home.*
They hold a friendly hand.
Thousands of friendly voices
Call across the crimson land.
There is a ring of brighter hope
Around the wintery moon
So, tell the children they will smile
When the wattles bloom.

2. *The rocky road was far too long.*
The shadows were too deep,
But they will sing a morning song

*With dancing in their feet.
For there is a ring of shining hope
Around the wintery moon
So, tell the children they will sing
When the wattles bloom.*

3. *Their lonely fires are flickering low
   Their Sacred Dream was dim.
   The ruthless sun was burning hot
   Along the wadi rim.
   But there is a brilliant ring of hope
   Around the silvery moon
   So, tell the children they will dance
   When the wattles bloom.*

4. *Tell the little laughing girl
   Near the emu watering hole
   The wattles are in golden bloom
   And she is golden loved.
   There is a brilliant ring of hope
   Around the silvery moon
   Tell the children they can dance
   Now the wattles bloom.*

> *Lyrics: Rod Cameron
> Music: Maria Rosa*

The aforementioned event occurred on 23 August 1989 when – together with speakers of First Nations descent, the Mount Saint Bernard students, singers and dancers from Mossman and Kuranda – Rod addressed 'The Eternal Now' and the meaning of 'The Dreaming' at the Civic Centre, Florence St, Cairns.

'Mapa Jarriya-Nyalaku'

A range of musically-oriented activities emerged in *Bidyadanga*/La Grange. A group of us formed a bush band with a most impressive lagerphone, tea chess bass, washboard and guitar combination. It played at 'Intermission' when evening screenings of films occurred on the community's basketball court. Children Activities Times Society (CATS) also presented several workshops which included puppetry. A holiday program sustained by older children helping younger ones with adult supervision created an enthusiastic embrace of the game 'Rob the Nest'. While visiting, Maurice Crocker (who later became ordained and a courageous advocate for survivors of sexual abuse) introduced this game to the young people. After he left, I suddenly found myself woken daily as soon as light dawned by children's voices whispering with compelling urgency through the veranda shutters: 'Miss Maria, Miss Maria! Rob the Nest! Rob the Nest!' They had come up from the camp to start the day joyously anticipating the game!

Once the game started (after my breakfast!) excitement would reach fever pitch and participants had a wonderfully happy time together. Yes, they laughed *'Deep joys of victory'*. As twilight fell and the evenings turned into night, we would often 'hear' a silent curtain rise with the beginning of traditional singing in the residents' first languages. The singing would float through the darkness as if searching and calling to the light. Rod's line: *'If the Dreaming dies, all human dreams grow dim'* profoundly speaks of this endeavour.

As part of an exercise associated with bushfire recovery in 2020, the group facilitator invited us to recall a time when we felt joy. This involved going back to a scene in our imagination then writing about it. Here is what I wrote:

One day at *Bidyadanga*/La Grange, we organise a class trip to the nearby Black Rock beach before lunch. When we arrive there, the sea water is milky. Though the tide is in, it is starting to turn. We stay on the sand until the outgoing momentum fully emotes. We know underwater rocks will become visible. Then we can go into the water and submerge ourselves completely for it is not stinger season. The water has no chill factor and the almost cloudless sky is such a vibrant blue!

It is beautiful to imbibe the whole scene and the happy faces of my class. My charges are running around playing 'chasey' (tag/tig/tiggy) while some cartwheel. In the distance, pelicans stand where the tidal creek enters the sea, looking like sentinels in suits. The sand stretches for kilometres far into the distance up and down the coast. No building whatsoever in sight!

We anticipate going out to the rocks when they appear and, with a stone, breaking open the rock oysters one at a time. It is a favourite pastime and communal meal. If the tide goes out far enough, we will check the fish trap and collect any fish in it to bring back to the community for the bereaved.

Even though they are young, my charges know this beach intimately. They are thoroughly at home and delight in all they see, the familiar and the new. I soak up their joy vicariously and suddenly recognised I also feel deep joy – because of their joy.

Indeed, these young people could be said to *'sing a morning song with dancing in their feet'*. Rod links the little laughing girl of the song 'La Grange'/ 'Dreamtime Music' to the one *'Near the emu watering hole'* in the song 'When the Wattles Bloom'. The word *Bidyadanga* is from a word for 'emu watering hole' (*pijarta* or *bidyada*).[14]

In the 1980s, at around the time of the 'bicentenary', a group of academics and students at Murdoch University began a conversation about the monument built in 1913 in commemoration of the death of three 'explorers' during a 1865 expedition at *Bidyadanga*/La Grange. In consultation with the *Karajarri* people and with permission from the Fremantle City Council, the group at Murdoch added a plaque that presents a counter-narrative about the expedition and details of the death of twenty Aboriginal people at the hands of Maitland Brown who led a 'punitive' expedition to return the remains of these 'explorers'. The plaque reads: 'This plaque is in memory of all the Aboriginal people killed at La Grange. It also commemorates the other Aboriginal people who died during the invasion of their country. Lest We Forget. Mapa Jarriya-Nyalaku.'[15]

'A land that's ancient and new'

CHAPTER 5

'STORYING'

BROLGA

Brolga was a girl for dancing
Down amid the spinifex.
She with graceful turning prancing
Was the envy of her sex.

Came a whirlwind from the mountain
Like a devil on the plain,
Down upon the girl in fury,
Brolga was not seen again.

Tribesmen came and searched in sorrow.
Wailing through the night was heard.
All they found on each tomorrow
Were the footprints of a bird.

Brolga, Brolga, bird of graces,
Ballerina turn and twirl!
Do your dance. Go through your paces,
Spirit of a vanished girl.

Repeat last verse.

Lyrics: Rod Cameron
Music: Maria Rosa

At Innisfail in 1987, Rod introduced the above song thus:

> Aboriginal stories can be very long and obscure and difficult for our European 'ear' to understand. Some of them are not. Many of them are very simple and very beautiful and one of the most popular ones concerns the brolga. These sacred stories have great depth. They are simple but deep. Simple things are usually the most profound.
>
> The brolga story is of a bird that dances in the morning. The bird is like a morning flower dancing in the morning time of life. The story starts with a girl who danced in the morning, a beautiful girl called Brolga. This was in the sacred creative time – a time translated in English sometimes as 'The Dreamtime'.
>
> Now this beautiful young woman symbolised all that is beautiful as she danced in the morning. Meeting a beautiful personality can become a morning time in our lives. We all know how beautiful young women are but Brolga, as a beautiful young woman, is a symbol of all that is beautiful and true regardless of how old the person is or whether they are male or female. Whenever I meet a beautiful personality, I am enriched; it gives me a new start in life, as though life has returned to the beginning time. Such a person becomes the morning of my life, giving me a new morning time. I am richer. My personality is richer from now on from having met you as such a person – you are beautiful regardless of how old you are or whether you are male or female.
>
> Brolga danced in the morning but there is evil in the world and the evil in this sacred story is represented by

a whirlwind that danced upon the plain. A whirlwind is an awesome spinning of the wind, a dust storm dancing across the plain. We have in this story the beautiful Brolga dancing as a symbol of all that is beautiful and true and we have this evil sweeping across the plain. There is a double dance and the evil is going to destroy the good and beautiful. And that's what happens. The whirlwind takes her away.

Young tribesmen go searching for her. Human life, the journey of human life is a search. We continue journeying, searching. Even when we possess the good and the beautiful, we search even more for them. The search becomes even more ardent. The search for the good and the beautiful is part of human life and it exists in this story of Brolga. The Brolga girl is immortalised in the symbol of the beautiful bird that dances on the plain. She is perpetuated in this way as a reminder to people. The bird is only a symbol. The whole story, the whole of creation is loaded with beautiful symbols that dance with meaning, and the little poem I wrote depicts this story.

James Cornell struggled with the problem of evil in the world. It horrified him that its machinations could exist alongside beauty and easily destroy it. Just as Brolga – the symbol of all that is beautiful in the world – could be lost, so many human beings experience betrayals, abandonment, scapegoating, malice, supremacy, unbridled rivalry, crucifying bullying and other forms of incarnated evil that compound the loss of life's purpose and meaning. Life is lost, becomes too hard, empty. René Girard wrote a challenging text addressing envy and dynamics named in this song. He links envy to 'mimetic desire'.[1]

Who Keeps Track?

Stories such as that of Battle Mountain and the *Kalkadoon* underline the existence of revenge attacks which amount to war crimes committed in the past settlement of Australia.[2] The consequent reality is that sometimes human beings do become *'Trapped like fish in a net'* of dispossession, oppression and powerlessness. Even though they know they are a human being with personal autonomy, First Nations people may experience an overwhelming sense of aloneness or alienation in relation to many other Australians. I wrote the song 'Our Tracker' with such scenarios in mind. In my appointment as a religious educator in another of the Special Government Schools for Aborigines due to my familiarity with church culture, using imagery students could relate to for wellbeing support became paramount.

OUR TRACKER

1. *The Lord is our tracker and He wants to follow,*
   Even though we're boss of wherever we go.

2. *Over the dust plains, flooded creeks and rivers,*
   I know He is there, tailing us.

3. *Winds of a cyclone can rage and blow,*
   Yet His presence and loving still can flow.

4. *And while on that journey to where we are going,*
   I know His Spirit cares for us.

5. *The Lord is our tracker and He wants to follow,*
   Even though we're boss of wherever we go

'STORYING'

I know He is there, tailing us
I know His Spirit cares for us
Even though we're boss of wherever we go.

Lyrics and Music: Maria Rosa

This song taps into the imagery and work of a 'tracker' familiar to many First Nations people and others. Drawing on the imagery of being pursued in a way similar to that expressed in Francis Thompson's poem 'The Hound of Heaven', James Cornell writes thus of encounter with the Absolute (inclusive of the Cosmic and Incarnated Christ or Loving Source of Life or Great Mystery):

> Gabriel Marcel, a twentieth-century French writer, proposed one of the most credible paths for approaching the Absolute. He said that reason could take us through the foothills of wonder to a height from which the eagle of faith could seize us and carry us to our heart's desire.
>
> I really admire Marcel's approach, but I later heard another version of the journey of faith that quite took my breath away with its accuracy and depth.
>
> An African elder was talking with a missionary and asked him what he understood as faith. 'It's about believing the right things about God and about life,' replied the missionary confidently.
>
> 'No,' said the elder. 'Faith is like a hungry lion. It roams the countryside tirelessly, seeking signs of prey, through day and through night, by scent and by sight till it comes within stalking distance. With infinite patience, using all its skills of concealment, it inches its way to within range. Then it charges with abandon and ferocious savagery till its prey is taken and beyond resistance.'

'You are right,' said the missionary, chastened. 'Faith is not a list of propositions. It is a constant, passionate and relentless search for the god in our lives.'

'You have missed the point,' said the elder, 'The lion is God.'³

The search for accessible imagery and a common meaning-making code in complex situations of heartache and brokenness where diverse cultures meet is necessary whether one is relating to the sacred or the secular.

As part of one school's religious education initiative, the staff decided to adopt the already existent concept of 'hero' as 'The Young Guy' which students regularly saw interpreted in many weekend movies imported into the town. The hero – especially in the Westerns – would usually be a brave young person dubbed 'The Young Guy'. So, Jesus came to be referred to as 'The Young Guy' within the Christian story. Jesus was of an age similar to the heroes seen working to mend 'thick' aspects of life. Anthropologists speak of obtaining 'thick' descriptions to access life's interacting layers. The person of Jesus thus was one, like many others who, consciously faced humanity's many-layered challenges within the international meeting places of the times. The writer Tony Swain claims the 'cult' of *Djulurru* to be the revamped image of Jesus as *Yangay* 'used to entice Aboriginal converts'.⁴ At the time I came across the term 'Young Guy' (almost twenty years before), it resided in the vernacular and referred to figures in many non-religious stories inspiring hope for meaningful resolutions of challenging situations portrayed in film. 'Young Guys' of all kinds captured imaginations via their responsive context-based actions addressing hardships experienced.

'STORYING'

Telling Stories[5]

Storytelling is an art form practised by many people around the world. Through it, knowledge and experiences are shared to reinforce life-enhancing connections with others. Artists try to do this in accessible formats. Stories may be centred around photographs, paintings on canvas or the body, a dance or a tattoo. Telling stories may remain predominantly oral in some cultural groups.

By participating in the art of storytelling, a transitional space can be entered where we may, ultimately, realise what is not said may be as powerful as what is. Stories held by written yarns, poems, prose, family histories, observations, experiences, fictionalised accounts or a song involve – as in other formats – writers grappling and giving voice to a part of life's immensity and diversity, its capacities and expressions within human beings, the natural world and ever-changing cultures. Deep questions can be touched upon, even regarding the nature of existence itself.

Artists work to find a form that best expresses what they need to say. Words have the potential to resonate, capture and provide a vehicle for this longing to communicate. Like other artists, writers allow themselves to be open to the emergence of the unknown in the actual transitional space of storytelling. They may wait for words to appear while simultaneously realising they need to subject themselves to the demands of the art form. In some ways, they are forever in training to take part in an act of creation and birth. Their works do not emerge fully-fledged from a production line. So, to begin, a writer may simply respond to Ernest Hemingway's invitation: 'All you have to do is write one true sentence. Write the truest sentence that you know.'

Any art form can be transportive, taking us into a zone where time melts, grasping parts of lives shaped in the past and holding them in the light of the transitional space of 'the now'. It can be integrative even though the process in which we engage may at times feel like a stumbling search, feeling our way through a mist to find the best way to tell the 'story'. With words, the writer brings a voice to and records observations of contexts in which they have participated, lived, celebrated, and even lost. The invisible yet powerful becomes visible.

By bringing attention to what has not yet been said, engaging in the art form of writing may be transformative. It can suggest outlines and present facts regarding past individuals, families, communities or other collective happenings which leave readers questioning versions of history they have been taught. Writing can give body to such facts, wings to hopes previously expressed, to imaginations as well as experiences. Writing can even act as a bridge between the closest of people as sometimes those standing closest may hold others in comfortable familiarity rather than clarity, a mirroring rather than a genuine meeting acknowledging difference.

Through shared stories, however, previously unrecognised negotiations others have had to make in transitional spaces mandating change may become apparent. Apart from recording happenings, stories encoded in the many forms of writing can give us insight into the use of power, and its impact on the personal lives of those who have, for example, lived under oppressive regimes. Any word from such histories that is 'heard' within ourselves or collectively by listeners/readers can be a catalyst for healing, gaining strength, and enhancing personal and even intergenerational recovery. Writings can celebrate humanity, especially its resilience. In the works of authors, we often find parts of ourselves echoing. Rod expresses much regarding the power of story in the following lyrics:

'STORYING'

STORY

Chorus:

If human hope is like a bird in flight,
Then story is in the air. It's where we live.

1. *Story fuels the fires of the soul*
   For when we find our theme, we find ourselves.

2. *The glorious universe is the mask of God*
   Worn not to conceal but to reveal.

Chorus

3. *God is the Meaning-Maker of the Cosmos*
   And every blade of grass holds Revelation.

4. *God speaks into the drama of our lives*
   In a manner that exceeds the reach of words.

Chorus

Lyrics: Rod Cameron
Music: Maria Rosa

Yunkaporta writes of the 'story-mind'.[6] Yarning circles produce potent effects.[7] Via 'yarning', complexity's layers emerge in a way that can be crystalline. The protocol for grounding the story-mind behind yarning is respect.[8]

$$$$ Story

The management of money, a seemingly mundane process, can become a drama in the lives of many. Though the administering of government funding in First Nations communities is a technically secular activity, it can be an expression of values deeply held. I had the opportunity to participate in helping community members manage community budgets via the creation of monthly 'Money Stories'. People could access displayed copies of the latter in everyday locations such as the store, clinic and community office noticeboards after they had been presented on large blackboards at a community meeting. At these everyday locations, people could leisurely restudy the information and refer to them whenever they felt the need.

The 'Money Story' method of communication regarding the evolving state of financial affairs (to which gifted former Community Development Advisors inducted both my husband Keis and I) ensured correct information flow reached all those needing to be aware of current levels of spending *vis-a-vis* pre-set budget lines. Instead of computer readouts whose content many could not grasp, the data became converted into green or red bar lines which indicated spending to date as correspondingly within budget or over. Facial expressions at the end of each red or green bar line graphically emphasised the state of affairs revealing the amount spent in relation to monthly allocations for the financial year. For example, sad – even crying – faces emphasised overspending. People realised overspent budget lines had to be compensated for by reining in spending in them or via an approved cutback of spending in others. I am not sure how much time I spent working as a volunteer on these elucidating graphics to ensure accurate communication flow. Often, the intensely image-oriented 'Money Story' copies would be finished in the small hours of the morning.

Much of their efficacy, however, depended on the promptness of hired accountants in generating and providing the information contained in monthly reports.

Instead of the words 'workers' compensation' for one budget line, an image of someone falling off a ladder stood beside the bar line showing how much insurance money had already been paid. Thus, similar images communicated to those who could not read what each budget line represented. Armed with the necessary information, people then would contribute to decisions regarding how community budgets could be balanced. This transparency relieved the community's Advisor of the onerous task of having to deny uninformed requests for resourcing funds from budget lines; it transferred accountability for all spending to councillors and community members. This empowering tool worked brilliantly. When in this instance contact with other Australians had only been for fifty years, translation of information into an accessible format necessary for the kind of deep knowledge needed to make informed decisions made an extraordinary difference. With sufficient information at hand, no-one needed directives telling them what to do, and how to manage their affairs. As time passed, this tool 'codifying the creative process … (used) manually' became an integrated software solution available in many locations.[9]

Why Warriors Pty Ltd has more recently worked for deep knowledge and informed decision-making concerning COVID-19 and other concerns for people in Arnhem Land.[10] Richard Trudgen, in one of their videos, notably claims that, from his decades' long observation of traditional ways, domestic violence did not feature in east Arnhem Land societies as five clans ensured the proper care of each person. He asserts domestic violence is where it is today 'because of the effects of colonisation'.[11] Is the anatomy of colonisation then an ongoing element needing closer scrutiny?

'Nothing About Us Without Us'

Although Keis had not envisaged having to spend so much time on the administration of money in his role as community Advisor, he firmly believed that good administration made a difference in the quality of people's lives. Two co-workers with previous experience in this role and the elders proved to be excellent sources of what we both needed to know. The elders, via their induction process on country, placed Keis' role within the context of their 'big picture' of life.[12] The elders and councillors with whom Keis worked made their own free, informed decisions and he understood his role as being part of their executive arm putting their decisions into practice.

Occasionally, Keis found himself unexpectedly being asked to speak to community outsiders on the elders' and councillors' behalf. This is because they recognised his distinct set of skills and abilities as complementing theirs at the time. I remember him saying he'd push back pointing out he thought speaking up was their role. However, at distinct times, the elders and councillors firmly insisted. Perhaps, since they had only had minimal contact with settlers for fifty years at the time, this proved to be one way they chose to observe another culture's ways of interacting in real-time and it was an instructive means of their becoming more bicultural. A similar rationale regarding participation in and overcoming any cultural constraints has been used via employing the *Milimika* circle in the school at *Wurrumiyanga* (formerly *Nguiu*) on the *Tiwi* Islands. 'When Tiwi people from different clan groups sit in a Milimika circle, everyone's voice is heard and considered.'[13] There a person with a distinctly valuable ability or connection is recognised and employed when needed.

Keis chose to support by agreeing to an occasional formal request from elders and councillors to advocate on their behalf but he insisted this action always be in their presence. Invariably, they briefed him beforehand so this was a consciously planned strategy on their part, not an assumed *modus operandi*. Some outsiders unaware of such a request did not fully grasp its existence and thus following through on the request at times proved 'tricky'.

It is important to be aware of gratuitous concurrence where First Nations people deal with 'interview' situations by simply agreeing with the interviewer. 'In mainstream settings, such as education, the law and the media, Aboriginal people know that it is advantageous to use "Anglo" ways of communicating.'[14] However, an advocate's role is to represent others no matter their personal viewpoint. The choice of an advocate belongs to those asking a person to relay their position. Know too, 'The skills involved in switching cultural styles are not automatic; it takes experience and time to learn them. The more a person successfully participates in other cultures, the greater is their chance of developing bicultural skills.'[15] At that time, a strong focus on observation proved to be one preferred way of cultivating them.

When someone asks you to advocate on their behalf, it is important to ensure permission to do so is given only concerning a specific issue at a specific time. Usually, the request emerges after consideration of many factors. Outsiders to a community do not help by infantilising those who made the request. Requests can occur at specific stages of intercultural negotiation and for different reasons. We need to continue to respect how people choose to enact the participatory principle of 'nothing about us without us'. The latter principle (originating with policymaking about people with disabilities) can readily be applied to the movement towards liberation for anybody at risk of being viewed through a deficit lens. Today, thankfully, many people not of Indigenous descent realise they need to learn how to develop services that effectively work for

Aboriginal people, ones which, for example, advocate on request and 'interpret silence appropriately'.[16]

Who is 'Boss'?

Sometimes people turned up in a remote community without its members having been formally notified of their intention to visit or explicitly doing any permit paperwork explaining their reason for visiting. Upon arrival, one man alighted from his car near where I stood with some young girls. He approached one of them and said, 'Hello. Who is your boss?' The lass spiritedly replied, 'I am boss of myself!' On another occasion, a fellow arrived and called an impromptu meeting of those within earshot. He wanted to talk about petrol sniffing. He had launched himself into the topic when a group of young men appeared on the fringes of the gathering. Their spokesperson interrupted the meeting saying, 'You are having a meeting and talking about us because we sniff petrol. Why did you not invite us? We do not like this.' Realising his oversight and the young people's valid objection, the man quickly left.

One First Nations remote Local Government Community Council formally articulated within their 'schedule' that a representative for all those who came from elsewhere to work had to be elected. This they saw as necessary because 'Workers who are not local have to live here too.' I found this most enlightened as it acknowledged the possibility of reverse discrimination happening – not allowing others to have a voice because they were 'outsiders'.

Unfortunately, the word 'boss' can trigger built-up residual feelings connected with being ordered or pushed around by representatives of a dominant culture, not being allowed to have any say or input into logistics affecting oneself. Sometimes a little thoughtfulness and planning can make a huge difference in such remote and very remote locations. A doctor appeared at the door of our classroom one Friday mid-morning and querulously asked: 'Where is everybody?' We replied the adults had gone to town (some hundreds of kilometres away) to do business in places that did not open on a Saturday. They would most likely not be back until after they had finished shopping and errands. I could almost see the steam coming out of the doctor's ears as he listened. He then told us, 'I have worked in Africa and there I am treated like a god. People there would always be lined up waiting for me – not like here!' We gently informed him community members travelled regularly to town via bus on a Friday. This established behaviour pattern is the reason we did not schedule work with them on Fridays. We chose to instead work longer hours on other days with interested people. He did not calm down however and stormed off. The question surfaced: Had adequate notice been given to allow for planning on the part of those who needed a weekly trip to town for supplies? If not, simply telling people you are coming through on a Friday without considering how they manage the remoteness of their situation and expecting them to change pre-organised plans without negotiation will likely be poor resource management.

This incident revealed a possible hierarchical system in operation. Much in such a system can be assumed which does not relate to local circumstances and patterns of living developed. In her thought-provoking text *Blood, Bones and Spirit*, Heather McDonald researched First Nations peoples' experiences of Christianity with fieldwork among *Gija* and *Jaru* in Halls Creek. She asserts:

> Late twentieth century Continental theologians, influenced by Western liberal democratic polities and

contemporary science, turned Western Christianity upside down and back to front. Western Christianity was dehierarchised and dehellenised, and feminised. God now is being un-kinged. His attributes of self-subsistence, transcendence and all power-knowledge are being jettisoned in favour of his relatedness to the whole of creation, including the experience of vulnerability and woundedness.[17]

She concludes: 'The religion that the missionaries preached to Aboriginal people was a religion of placelessness which developed its utopian qualities in diaspora and exile. ... On bush trips ... one not only hears stories of station life and contemporary life but also stories of the Dreamtime. ... Rather than accepting a religion of exile (that is, a salvation religion) as a compensation for dispossession and displacement, Aboriginal people in northern Australia are choosing to repossess their land instead.'[18]

In seeking the essence of movement within cultural spaces under consideration, we cannot dismiss the fact First Nations peoples relate via the land to beings that reside in their particular equivalent of *Alcheringa/Tjukurrpa*. In speaking to youth in the following song, *Kiata* (a Spirit Person ... the Spirit of fire, light and heat ... the Spirit of Summertime. ... the Flame) affirms a First Nations perspective. We cannot allow any youth to believe their people's ways of explaining and negotiating life are to be completely devalued and discarded.

'STORYING'

WILL ALL THE CAMPFIRES FAIL?

(Youth:) Kiata, will all the campfires fail?
Will they go out? (Spoken)

(Kiata:)   No! No!

1. *No, my young ones, that could never be*
   All the deep world cries for their survival
   It would be easier to extinguish all the stars
   Or to rob the majestic moon of its solemnity.

2. *This night is dark*
   But deepest dreams are born of darkest nights
   Already I can hear the call of dawn
   I can see the cry of sunrise in your eyes
   I can see the cry of sunrise in your eyes

3. *The fires will never fail*
   For the spirit of youth will burn when morning comes
   The spirit of youth will burn when morning comes
   When morning comes.

            Lyrics: Rod Cameron
            Music: Maria Rosa

Different Ways

In supporting First Nations people aspiring to run a store, the anthropologist, missionary and community Advisor Margaret Bain had the insight to explain – when they failed – that their way of managing affairs simply differed. She said once she pointed this fact out, the hats (lowered to hide their eyes) raised and those involved stood taller. These key people who had tried valiantly to succeed realised that running the community store according to mainstream business principles seemed 'like we have no relations'. Her proposal for future business projects underlined the importance of what she called 'gears'.[19] When a situation emerged in which kinship obligations could jeopardise the flow of money to keep a project afloat, she recommended another model be used, such as others not kinned being formally invited into the dynamic. This meant changing 'gears' so freedom to say 'no' would enable more meaningful kinship-based interactions to still continue.

Creating similar workplace models respectful of First Nations perspectives has ensured greater cultural safety and positive outcomes in situations as on the *Tiwi* Islands where the previously mentioned *Milimika* Circle has operated. The following song inspired by the standard Christian Lord's Prayer speaks to the brokenness unwittingly created when 'strange', different ways are devalued or discarded.

PRAYER FOR CREATION

1. *Creator, we sing to You*
   Sustainer on this earth.
   You call us to custodianship
   Of its flourishing and rebirth.

   Give us this day our daily bread
   Feed us in the Word that is said.
   Step into our brokenness,
   Heal in forgiveness.

2. *Creator, You touch us in our pain*
   Call to your people again.
   Ever as stranger You knock at our doors
   And hope that it's not in vain.

   Give us this day our daily bread[20]
   Feed us in the Word that is said.
   Step into our brokenness,
   Heal in forgiveness.
   Step into our brokenness,
   Heal in forgiveness.
   Heal in forgiveness.
   Heal in forgiveness.

   Lyrics and Music: Maria Rosa

Surprisingly retiring while at the top of her game in 2022, tennis star Ash Barty has sought to nourish her connections with Indigenous Australia. Her comment: 'There's no right way, there's no wrong way …it's just my way,' supports Margaret Bain's explanation to the crestfallen elders.

'cosmetic desert dust'

CHAPTER 6

'NOT FAR FROM OODNADATTA'

BLACK MADONNA

Black Madonna of the earth,
Robed in soil and tatter.
Symbol of perennial birth
Not far from Oodnadatta,
Not far from Oodnadatta.

You dignify your bark windbreak
Cosmetic desert dust.
Watch the blood red dawn awake,
As black madonnas must,
As black madonnas must.

Caress and kiss the precious soil,
Spirit lives in matter.
Labour in maternal toil,
Not far from Oodnadatta,
Not far from Oodnadatta.

Lyrics: Rod Cameron
Music: Maria Rosa

Rod Cameron explained the genesis of the poem on which this song is based:

> Some years ago, I had the privilege of travelling. I rode on the Old Ghan train from Port Augusta to Alice Springs. The old train track has since been abandoned. The Ghan now travels through Coober Pedy. The old track of the train was called after the Afghan camel drivers who pioneered that route. That old train route had many attractive features. You could get out of the train then and walk along the Birdsville Track for a while (before reboarding the train for its continuing northward run to Alice Springs* *brackets mine*). That's a bit of an experience. The Birdsville Track played a very important part in the history of this part of the Australian Outback.
>
> The old train 'The Ghan' was very comfortable and luxurious inside. It ran very slowly along the southern fringe of Lake Eyre. Lake Eyre is in two parts and this part fringed the southern end of it. While onboard, you could see a vast wasteland of grey-white, lifeless plains as far as the eye could see. Truly it brought home to me part of the grimness and the cruelness of Australia. It also emphasised part of the greatness of this land for me. The train, having skirted Lake Eyre, turned northward across the gibber plain. That is truly a sight to see – endless horizons of sweeps of little red rocks and seemingly lifeless land. Then the train went on to Oodnadatta, a little town struggling in the sun. On the outskirts of Oodnadatta, I saw a little young Aboriginal woman sitting with her baby in a windbreak, just those two inside a few branches positioned to keep the wind at

bay. On the train from Oodnadatta up to Alice Springs, I wrote this little poem called 'Black Madonna'.[1]

In Australia in the past, much earlier mentioned work done by First Nations people kept many non-Indigenous-owned enterprises, such as remote stations, afloat. Often, however, the lifetime needs of Indigenous women who provided company for non-Indigenous men were societally ill-met or treated as if they were invisible.

Tellingly: 'The narrator of *Invisible Man* (a novel by Ralph Ellison, published in 1952) is a nameless young black man who moves in a 20th-century America where reality is surreal and who can survive only through pretense. Because the people he encounters "see only my surroundings, themselves or figments of their imagination", he is effectively invisible. He leaves the racist South for New York City, but his encounters continue to disgust him. Ultimately, he retreats to a hole in the ground, which he furnishes and makes his home.'[2]

When I read Rod's poem written on The Ghan, it spoke to me of the dignity he saw in the 'little young Aboriginal woman'. It was not invisible. Now, after reading Lowitja O'Donoghue's authorised biography, I cannot help associating Oodnadatta with the heartbreak of her mother Lily O'Donoghue who had five children fathered by Mick O'Donoghue (owner of Granite Downs pastoral station at one time) taken from her by missionaries. Lily later took the surname Woodforde, had more children, and became a 'drinker'.[3] When Lowitja tried to find her, she learned her mother lived in Oodnadatta.

When Lily hears her daughter is coming to meet her after their forced separation of thirty-three years, 'she waits, at the edge of town, staring off into the desert, day after day, from early morning until sundown'.[4] This she did for weeks 'from first light in the morning'.⁵ When they do finally meet again, Lowitja is thirty-five years old but neither of them speaks the other's language.

Lily is most concerned that Lowitja and her sister Eileen do not see where she lives. On a return trip to Oodnadatta however, Lowitja asks where her mother is and 'finds her living in a scrap-iron wurlie on a treeless flat'.⁶ Remembering this occasion, Lowitja says, 'My mother was a broken woman living in appalling conditions and it is obvious the hurt she suffered by the removal of five of her children.'⁷ 'Later when she speaks of the reunion, as she often will, Lowitja will say that it taught her about the limitlessness of hope and the strength of patience: "I learnt what hope and patience mean – how she had never given up hope of seeing her children again. I also learnt what kinship means to Aboriginal people – how in traditional society everyone has a place and a relationship with all other members of the group. From my mother I also realised what it was to be on the receiving end of racist policies and to have basic human rights denied".'⁸ 'I guess the thing that upsets me most is what my mother went through, all those years. I feel quite angry at the mission authorities for not at least sending some photographs so that she could know what we looked like.'⁹ A crucial question for me is: 'What does moving human rights from abstraction mean?'

Lily died on 17 October 1979. Unable to travel for a traditional funeral in Lily's home country at *Iwantja*/Indulkana because the road is blocked by 'men's business' ceremonies, Eileen, Lowitja and the family decide to bury her at Oodnadatta in the sandhills outside the town. 'No hymns are sung and no prayers are said. There is no ceremony of any kind. Afterward, Eileen and Gordon drive south to Quorn, and Lowitja flies north to Alice Springs, and the wind blows across the sandhills until they can't remember where they buried her.'¹⁰

Like the *Invisible Man*, Lily's remains have a hidden home. What a sad and heart-wrenching story when we consider what may have otherwise been possible in and through life if she had encountered interpathy! The line: *'As black madonnas must'* hints of the abominably harsh treatment experienced and the minimal level of choice allowed in the past to mothers like Lily. Is not being structurally affirming of all their dignity relevant?

The non-Indigenous writer Paul Barnsley described his experience of covering confronting media stories related to Canada's Indigenous people for over twenty-five years as like 'going through the looking glass'. 'A reference to a world where things are not as they should be. Where known rules no longer apply.'[11] In speaking about the removal of children for placement in institutions, a Canadian Indigenous elder is recorded as saying, 'The schools were never meant to do us any good. They knew. They knew that when you break the hearts of our women, you break the strength of our nations.'[12] Despite good intentions and some benefits as side effects, we need to ask ourselves deep questions about removal from place and kin and other policies. Were these ultimately designed to erase other perspectives? The perspectives of people who already had rights to live in places like Canada and Australia? The concrete application of the United Nations Declaration on the Rights of Indigenous Peoples will hopefully become better understood in the interdependent creation of our future.

Even though Lily O'Donoghue (aka Woodforde) lived near Oodnadatta on a treeless plain, I choose to imagine her sitting like those in this song, dreaming hope in her native *Yankunytjatjara*. At other times, surely the pain of the loss of five of her children drove her to the self-medication of excessive alcohol use.

PAPERBARK TREES
*(Alternative name: **AT CAMP**)*

And still they sit and dream,
They will forever dream,
In the shade of the paperbark trees,
In the shade of the paperbark trees.

As wordless as the mist,
Their thoughts are as the mist,
In the shade of the paperbark trees,
In the shade of the paperbark trees.

In rows of dreaming clouds,
These people of the clouds,
In the shade of the paperbark trees,
In the shade of the paperbark trees.

For time is in eternity,
And eternity in time,
In the shade of the paperbark trees,
In the shade of the paperbark trees.

> *Lyrics: Rod Cameron*
> *Music: Ron Bopf*

In more traditionally influenced First Nations contexts, women can contribute to the decision-making which impacts their lives. Elders can discuss options, for example, using 'fire-politics' as described by author Zohl Dé Ishtar below. Though not Indigenous, she assisted in the set-up and running of the women's camp (*Tjilimi*), *Kapululangu* Women's Law and Culture Centre, and came to comprehend 'just how deeply ingrained White racism runs within the psyche of even the most well-meaning Whitefellas'.[13]

> 'Fire politics' is a circular decision-making process which relies on Indigenous horizontal governance and replaces White hierarchical dictates. As Kapululangu's co-ordinator, I quickly learned that meetings did not happen – not in the White sense – and that decision-making was neither straight-forward, nor certain. As a result, most of our 'meetings' consisted of chatting around the *waru* (the *Tjilimi* fire), usually over breakfast or late at night. Someone would raise an issue, which was talked about briefly then circulated organically through impromptu one-to-one and small group discussions over a period of several days and then the discussion returned to the *Tjilimi* fire where the matter would be further discussed. Although I was often part of these discussions as part of their rounds, it is only after this process had been completed that, if the elders thought it was appropriate, the decision would be relayed to me (formally or informally) at our communication nexus: the *waru*. This unique process enabled all who should be involved to have an opportunity to contribute. It ensured that decision-making control was held by the elders and that nothing that happened under the rubric of Kapululangu occurred without the elders' agreement.[14]

Such a process ensures ownership and powerful sustainability of decisions made as distinct from 'solutions imposed' from elsewhere. Ochre Doyle on the back cover of Ishtar's text exhorts us: 'It is our responsibility to learn how internalised racism poisons Aboriginal lifeworlds as surely as kero poisoned waterholes and strychnine poisoned flour.'

'I can see the cry of sunrise'

CHAPTER 7

BEYOND 'TINSEL' BINARIES

FRINGE DWELLER

She gives her smiling eyes to all,
Bitterness too young to know,
As yet she has not come to feel
Sorrow's acid edge.

Her grandad and the broken stump
Aborted, broken dreams,
Are bereft of Dreaming they can share,
Nightmare, endless night.

Twilight people seek a way,
Groping from within,
A grow-back moment's dawning search
For a remnant of their Dream.

O little Fringe Dweller, O little one,
O little Fringe Dweller,
Keep walking towards the sun.
Keep walking towards the sun.

Lyrics: Rod Cameron, James Cornell
Music: Maria Rosa

Unprocessed pain not faced collectively lives on. The Australian author Richard Flanagan in speaking with Laura Tingle at The Sydney Writers' Festival names Tasmania (where his birthplace, his 'soul country' is) as a completely different country. He asserts for a quarter of its modern history Tasmania has suffered from two major traumas: its invasion with nearly successful genocide of its Indigenous people and a slave system rooted in convictism which meted out labour as modelled by the plantation system in the Caribbean. Due to mass traumas like these around the world, he speaks of the possibilities of persisting 'pathologies'.[1] Flanagan and Tingle consider the status many experience of being on the edges/the fringes, and how a novel can seek to define the universal in the particular.[2]

Although I heard of First Nations people when my family moved to Gippsland, I only realised the composition of their fringe status more fully after going north. Until then, I simply assumed their fringe status fell into the same category and had the same composition *vis-a-vis* the mainstream 'Anglo' culture as that of non-Anglo emigrants to this land. Grappling with the meaning of being Australian, we discover the traumas of transported convicts, young boys in the United Kingdom sent here away from their parents, post-World War II displaced persons, refugees, the Stolen Generation and other Indigenous groups. Their experiences haunt them and, only via bringing all into the light or truth-telling, can we truly reimagine our future together. Interestingly, Richard Flanagan in the same conversation with Laura Tingle brings to our attention the special extra tense present in the *Yolŋu* language of *Miwatj*/north-east Arnhem Land.[3]

A defining moment of the relegation of First Nations realities to the fringe impacted me at the opening ceremony of a new church. My teaching role including religious education and coordinating in the local school meant I attended it as did quite a number of the school students. During the ceremony, the presiding church authority told those present: 'From now on there are no more sacred places. This is THE sacred place.' After the service had finished, the students and I filed out via the side door. When we got outside, one of the older children asked me: 'Miss Maria, what did that man mean when he said there are no more sacred places?' Should you think children are not paying attention to what older people say and do – especially in church – please beware! I looked at the other students who met my eyes with troubled faces. I did not know I would be called upon to answer such a question and felt close to panic. The official's words had troubled my heart too.

Faced with displaying both loyalty to the church authority and acknowledgement of the children's heritage, I looked them straight in the eye and said as lightly as I could, 'Oh, don't worry about it!' I did not wish to alarm them any further. I realised, however, that how I answered this question for myself would be crucial. Unprepared and feeling inadequate in managing more constructively what had occurred, I felt on the edge of a precipice, unable to go forward. Could I buy myself time as a young person myself? Learn more about how to negotiate this situation? As I scanned my mind for reference points and valid words to address this question more comprehensively and satisfactorily, one of the leaders of First Nations descent also exited via the same door. I greeted him as he walked past us. He tried to respond but the words did not come out. They seemed to catch in his throat. I realised he was in pain – not one for which calling an ambulance would do any good. The children saw this too.

Shaken, I made an appointment to speak with one of the visiting ceremony concelebrants. I wished to seek an outsider's point of view hoping it may give me a solid guiding touchstone. He listened attentively to my dilemma, shook his head, and then just said, 'Maria, remember. Christ is greater than the church.' It sounded to me like he had no other answer for me. Perhaps he also had the same dilemma? What could I do to answer the children's question authentically? Here, in stark reality, I had witnessed the seemingly perfunctory total dismissal of their people's way of being, the understanding of their place within the cosmos, and their vision of life. I temporarily swallowed my doubts and what some may now call cultural sensitivity. I kept doing my job as best as I could. I sought to acknowledge the gifts already within those who understood themselves to be in a different relationship with land than the church authority figure claimed for them. I focused on learning the *lingua franca* which played a significant role in the bilingual curriculum.

However, my troubled heart would not be denied. After speaking with someone on my Christmas break who had worked in Indonesia, I did not return to work the following year – only to pack up my possessions. I cried as I left in a small plane watching the country unfold before me from the air, grieving. It would cost me too much personally to continue living into an existence of endeavouring to conform to what I saw as a destructive status quo simply because it was advocated by authority. So, despite my love for the place, its people, and my teaching duties, I chose to leave. Initially, I had been drawn to working there because of my interest in bilingual/bicultural education. Years later, I met a similar worrisome invalidation by a member of another denomination.

After leaving the above community, I did some medical receptionist work at a Melbourne hospital until one day the Matron said to me: 'Maria, are you going to be doing this for the rest of your life? If not, there is a bursary being offered to study in Sydney for which I would like to recommend you. What say you?' Thus began my further study to answer some of my burning questions about those deemed by some to dwell on the fringes of 'salvation'.

Not only did First Nations people live on the fringes between 'everlasting damnation' and the promise of 'salvation', but they also hung about on the fringes of the homes of mainstream folk! They were 'moved on' whenever caught newly released from prison without a bed, shower or meal. A thoughtful dedicated group I came across in one capital city imagined an old building converted into a Women's Night Shelter would provide a safe place for them. One mid-morning, however, a couple of men knocked on its door and asked for one of the women sheltering by name. When they detected hesitancy to answer on the part of the worker, both of them assured her they simply wished to check on the woman's welfare. The worker said she did not know if the lady was still in but she'd check. She told the woman of the men's presence at the front door. The woman asked for time to climb the back fence! Slowly making her way back to the front door, the worker invited the men in to have a look around the facility. The woman they wished to see however had disappeared.

Some association triggered alarm in this homeless woman the next time she came to stay. She grabbed a knife and bailed all the workers up against a wall. Fortunately, one of the volunteers on duty had a magnificent sense of humour and defused the situation. He talked her into laying down the knife. All then ended up having a cup of tea together – with plenty of sugar! That night we learned how the effects of trauma previously experienced can manifest and the need for their recognition. While not condoning threatening behaviour, clearly some women are homeless due to violence already experienced and searingly registered in them. Elsewhere, I witnessed a similar defusion of an unarmed person. A colleague calmed her down by asking her to look into his eyes. The colleague then said he was going to wrap a hand around each of her wrists and hold on tightly. In this way, she gradually calmed down.

Seeking Refuge

We may have heard of self-medication, of how people seek to dull pain by drinking to excess or in other ways. I met a Native American woman who asked me how I managed my grief after the death of my beloved husband. She disclosed to me that, after she lost hers, she could not eat and survived by drinking whisky. Only via a friend's caring connection did she recover to the degree that she could function in other ways she said.

At a taxi stand in New York, I struck up a conversation with a Native American man standing behind me in the queue. He told me that, if he related seriously to the way he daily experienced being treated as 'a lesser human being', he would 'go mad'. I have seen many seeming to seek refuge from such a sense of alienation. This song connects with this reality. Rod Cameron again has *Kiata*: 'a Spirit Person ... the Spirit of fire, light and heat ... the Spirit of Summertime. ... the Flame' speaking:

KIATA TO KI-IN-KUMI

1. *Ki-in-kumi, listen to me!*
   You have grovelled in this riverbed too long.
   What you drink is deadly to you.
   It is shattering you like glass
   and your life-blood stains the earth.

2. *You are by birth a man of wide horizons*
   and yet upon this gravel bed you lie
   as though content to die!
   All song has faded from your dribbling lips,
   all visions from your eyes.

3. *If you were hopeless, I would leave you here*
   to drink yourself into oblivion
   But deep within you burns an ancient fire
   that cannot be easily quenched.

4. *Anyone who does not know the Spirit*
   that burns in the deepest caverns of your soul
   does not know you, Ki-in-kumi!
   Does not know you, Ki-in-kumi!

   Anyone who does not know the Spirit
   that burns in the deepest caverns of your soul
   does not know you, Ki-in-kumi!

5. *You have the answer in you, and you know it,*
   Smash your prison into broken glass.
   Take on the strength of rock!
   Stand and walk!

6. *Do it for yourself and for your people.*
   Do it for the nation old and new!
   Let all the people praise you!
   Let all the people praise you!

7. *If the Dreaming dies all human dreams grow dim.*
   So, Ki-in-kumi, stand and walk!

   Lyrics: Rod Cameron
   Music: Maria Rosa

Fire Wrapped in Stone is the title of the album in which this song resides. This title refers to the fire enabling us to choose to move toward reality-based, life-enhancing practice. From Benedictine monk Brother Steindl-Rast's experiences which included growing up as a teenager under Hitler, he states: 'The mystic is not a special human being. Every human being is a special kind of mystic.'[4] He elaborates further:

> The religions start with mysticism. There is no other way to start a religion. But compare this to a volcano that gushes forth ... and then ... the magma flows down the side of the mountain and cools off. And when it reaches the bottom, it's just rocks. You'd never guess that there was fire in it. So after a couple of hundred years, or two thousand years or more, what once was alive is dead rock. Doctrine becomes doctrinaire. Morals become moralistic. Ritual becomes ritualistic. What do we do with it? We have to push through the crust and go to the fire that's within it.[5]

He also refers to Raimon/Raimundo Panikkar who said, 'the future will not be a new, big tower of power. Our hope in the future is ... well-trodden paths from house to house.'[6]

'Whitefellas' – Identifier Term/White-Black Binary

I will now share with you an alienating experience published in 2010 by John Bradley, a person not of Australian First Nations descent who also found himself with the responsibility of teaching many Aboriginal students attending compulsory school education.[7] The telling 1980 incident described by him occurred in Borroloola. It can challenge perceptions of relationships. Bradley had intentionally been learning the language of the *Yanyuwa* people among whom he found himself. Meeting some of them on the way to withdraw money from the local banking agency, he greeted them and began a conversational ebb and flow in which he trialled some of what he had learnt. All ended up laughing together. This exchange seemed to infuriate one of the local non-Indigenous workers, who Bradley writes 'slammed a tin of black Nugget shoe polish on the counter and said, "That's the only thing you can have from this place. Just go and paint yourself!" and strode off. I stood waiting, in shock, until another person served me, the atmosphere uncomfortable with unspoken thoughts – something between "You get what you deserve" and "Don't worry about it: that's just the way life is at Borroloola sometimes." '[8]

Bradley explains in his text that the minority white population controlled all the resources at the time and used the privileged currency which knowledge of English afforded them. 'Yet they seemed ill equipped and uneasy in Borroloola. It was as if some power had thrown a whole lot of different people from the urban heartlands of Australia into this remote place just to see what would happen. The result was every kind of ignoble behaviour: jealousy, small-mindedness, racism, ignorance, entangled love affairs, madness, deep sorrow, bitchiness, paranoia, Christian evangelising – all, more than not, expressing the colonialist imperative that the white man is always boss.'[9]

He shares that after the incident: 'A part of me was raging, not only against the racism of the person at the counter, but also at my rejection as a community member because of the way I interacted with Yanyuwa people. I had long felt that racism was a shallow and ignorant response to others who were just different, but I did not expect racist retribution for taking the trouble to learn their language.'[10]

Here the content of an accusatory, demeaning, unfair 'white-black' binary rears its head despite the local people endeavouring to fit in and work with others. They chose to build a meaningful human relationship with a 'white' person who sought to understand their perspective and worldview via language learning. Reading what a person who is not of Aboriginal or Torres Strait Islander descent experienced living in this in-between space, we can only imagine what it is like for a person of Aboriginal or Torres Strait Islander descent to negotiate it. What a weight to carry!

I have heard the term 'inner sanctum' used by a person of non-Indigenous descent to describe the safe space where endeavouring to hold complex cultural realities fairly is respected and valued. Some of the complexity is exemplified by an incident in a remote community office where a community Advisor (aka Council Clerk in the NT) listened as a senior elder animatedly spoke into the phone. He used his first language yet, now and then, the Advisor noted the word *whitefella* sprinkled his speech. Noticing the tone of the conversation, the Advisor felt compelled to say, 'Hang on (using a term of respect for a male elder)! I'm a *whitefella* too!' The elder paused, thought for a moment then turned to him and said in his language: 'No! You are black!' Then he continued talking to the person on the other end of the phone line, once again peppering what he needed to say with the word *whitefella*. What had the elder just strongly emphasised in his language?

In this exchange, the elder declared that the Advisor did not fit into the meaning of his use of the Aboriginal English word *whitefella*. If we use skin tone and heritage to determine 'whiteness', the Advisor certainly correctly identified himself. However, the elder's contradiction of these identifiers underlined a very important distinction in the meaning he attributed to the word *whitefella*. In this elder's mind, skin tone and heritage had nothing to do with being described as a *whitefella*. His use of this word described someone outside the sphere of meaning in which he operated. Defining someone as 'black' in his language meant the elder saw the person as someone who understood his perspective, acted in a way validating the involvement of community members in decision-making, and upheld those decisions in consequent actions. It spoke of the Advisor's congruence with the context – a remote community of predominantly First Nations people. Here the *whitefella* system was one which needed to stand starkly in dialogue with a majority 'black' perspective ultimately reached via creating consensus. Anyone who did not seriously respect the process of dialogue with a 'black' perspective and follow through on results achieved, differentiated themselves as a *whitefella*, someone over and against.

Kylie Captain describes her identity as coming from within: 'I'm often told I don't look Aboriginal and people often ask what percentage I am – which I find extremely offensive. As Blackfullas we don't go by what percentage we are. It's not about the colour of my skin, it's about the culture and heritage which runs through my blood.'[11] The meeting place of cultures consequently needs to be a nuanced one. The white-black binary based on skin tone has the potential to create permanently crushing barriers and fringe dwellers of First Peoples by default – a minority versus majority situation.

Who Remembers What on 26 January?

On 26 January 1988 while out walking in Sydney, I came across a march to commemorate 'Invasion' or 'Survival Day'. The marchers protested against the equating of Australia Day with the dismissal of Indigenous pain associated with 'Year Zero'. They celebrated the survival of their people since 'Year Zero' in Australia. The remnant referred to in the following song represents the survivors, the unobliterated who fought and continue to fight against the mentality that the needs of all First Nations people can be summed up by the expression: 'soothing of the dying pillow'.[12]

DANCING SPIRIT

Chorus:

A remnant, sacred, gracing,
A remnant, sacred, gracing,
A remnant, sacred, gracing,
Came to dance its spirit.
Came into the city,
Came into the city,
Came into the city,
And danced its spirit.

1. *Looking round with wonder*
   Looking wonder from their eyes.
   Dancing sacred thunder
   Down expectant tinsel lies.

2. *Clothes hanger people*
   Hurrying by
   Momentarily turn and start,
   Stirred to ancient reverie
   By this vision of the naked heart.

   Chorus

3. *Ancient parent culture*
   Ancient parent roof
   Recalling adult restless children
   To the secret of their youth.

> *Lyrics: James Cornell*
> *Music: Maria Rosa, 11 April 1988*

Desert resurrection

CHAPTER 8

'HARVEST HAPPINESS'

FIREGLOW

Chorus:

Fireglow, heart glow, fireglow
Heart glow, let go, let go
At home, at home, sheltered
We are sheltered, sheltered, sheltered from the storm.

1. *Miles of mystic welcome window glow*
   The blue that haunts the evening air
   Enters inside a man
   And plays upon the strings of loneliness there
   Home is where you're understood
   The springtime of a brother's smile.

2. *Nearing empty flagon*
   Warmth and symbol of my soul
   Nothing more than old bough sheds
   That we can call our own.
   Yet in all this knowing
   That a house is not a home
   And the wind is not the worst that is around.

3. *I'm longing for a homeland*
    A home I've never known
    Longing for a fire
    Beyond the call of mind
    For dignity and presence
    The comfort of my kind
    The springtime of a sister's smile
    Bringing summer harvest happiness.

4. *Seeking for a space*
    For a vision of the sky
    For a sense of true belonging
    For an 'our' sense of 'my'
    Longing for deliverance
    From a whirlpool stranglehold
    Longing for a home
    For my body and for my soul.

Lyrics: James Cornell
Music: Maria Rosa

The initial inspiration for the above song came from James Cornell's poem called 'Sanctions' in which he describes the plight of a woman facing the coming winter in Rome after four months of homelessness.[1] He wrote: '(She) lived in a public park in Rome, in a hut made from cardboard boxes and plastic. I visited her often as a prelude to helping a group of concerned citizens help her relocate to a boarding house. Her refrain was constant: "God will give me justice against the one who has reduced me to this." '[2]

The song's lyrics also include references to Indigenous realities. Counteracting the degree of homelessness among First Nations people in various parts of Australia, the living conditions on the fringes of towns and cities, and the sense of alienation from mainstream societies, the Homeland/Outstation movement has stood as remedying dispossession of a sense of being at 'home'. Since 'The Intervention' and the *Stronger Futures* legislation cemented the changes initiated by the Federal Government in 2007, has the upkeep of homelands been deprioritised? This question needs attention. The composition of this song blossomed as some high school students in Sydney prepared to work at Woolloomooloo's Matt Talbot Hostel for the Homeless as part of their Community Service subject. The students asked me if they could experiment with singing this song and create their musical arrangement (not recorded by me). It turned out to beautifully reflect their spirit.

Reality of Trauma

At another school, a traditional healer – a *nangkari* – approached me. She said, 'Maria, the spirits of the children in that school are outside their bodies. They need healing.' I asked, 'What can we do about it?' She replied, 'We need to do a smoking ceremony for each class and their teachers. It will not do any good unless the teachers come too.' She had just described what I had learnt in yet another context – that spirits 'outside the body' is a way some First Nations people speak of the lingering effects of trauma either experienced or being experienced. The practice of the *nangkari* spoke to the necessary recognition of these effects.

When a young man came in off the street and asked if he could attempt computing, one of my First Nations colleagues abruptly left the room. As the young man and I proceeded to engage the intricacies of a computer, I realised he struggled through a fog created by prescribed medication. Yet, he persisted and broke through to achieve a good IT (Information Technology) outcome. During the scheduled break, I learned from my colleague that she had unfortunately been present at an incident in which he had been the victim of severe physical violence. Here I came face-to-face with the effects on him and her vicarious trauma.

Holding More than One 'Year Zero'

The renewal of a USA visa required my complete departure from the North American continent before being allowed to return to finish the International Trauma Studies Program (ITSP) offered by Columbia University's Mailman School of Public Health in New York. The time of my departure coincided with a biennial Practical Theology conference being held in Europe. Having attended a previous conference as a visitor, I sought to attend it under a similar banner. While fulfilling the USA conditions for re-entry, I thus had the opportunity to hear more scholars presenting research papers relevant to my doctoral thesis' foundational discipline.

I had chosen to research the thesis topic in perspectives afforded via the discipline of Practical Theology. As I understood it then and still do, Practical Theology is open to dialogue with the social as well as sacred sciences. Though this conference did not have representatives of First Nations peoples presenting or attending, I still thought it worthwhile hearing the scheduled presentations on 'Trauma and Spirituality' in particular alongside perspectives afforded by other Christian denominational involvements. The occasion presented a fruitful way of hearing ecumenically-informed concerns while attending to visa requirements.

Evidence of Australians from First Nations speaking from within various Christian denominations is provided by the 'theology in process' recorded by the Rainbow Spirit Elders.[3] Remote communities of predominantly First Nations peoples in Australia have had significant contact with the various Christian denominations over the years and the long-term educator Richard Trudgen based in Arnhem Land had already asserted the study of the impacts of trauma individually, collectively and intergenerationally to be sadly lacking in the field of Aboriginal health.[4] He maintained that 'we are dealing with severely traumatised people' in Arnhem Land and 'Much of the stress and trauma ... is the result of past trauma replayed and therefore re-traumatising the people in the continuing devastating relationship between Yolŋu and the dominant culture.'[5] This can be said of other First Peoples too. Rachel Perkins describes colonisation as 'a word that cannot hope to capture the cataclysmic shift ... luminaries of Central Australia have experienced in their lifetime'.[6]

Conference attendees had the option of visiting Auschwitz via one of the planned excursions. Many of us had already visited a site that sheltered some needing medical care during WWII. From the interpretative guidance given, WWII and its realities started to impinge more concretely on my consciousness. On one of my walks in Berlin after conference sessions, I came across the grave of Dietrich Bonhoeffer at *Dorotheenstadtischer und Friedrickswereder Friedhof.* Two weeks before the Allies marched into Flossenbürg, its camp officials hanged Bonhoeffer as a conspirator against Hitler to whom the German church it is claimed capitulated in the 1930s. In 1981, I read Bonhoeffer's *Letters and Papers from Prison* and had, ever since, maintained a strong interest in his ideas on 'religionless Christianity' and 'costly grace'. I had booked my accommodation for the duration of the conference at a freshly renovated venue called Hotel *Dietrich Bonhoeffer Haus* at *Ziegelstrasse 30.*

When the time arrived to set out on the excursion to Auschwitz, I decided not to go. My father spent much of WWII in two concentration camps run by German officers. I lived closely with the subsequent effects of his internment and being caught in the Allies' bombing of Germany. The thought of seeing one of the camps where the multiplication of these effects on others originated weighed heavily on me. From my work in Australian Indigenous Affairs, I had learned the necessity of taking breaks and not asking too much of ourselves, especially when others' expectations may be operating. This is why I did not go to Auschwitz. There are times when it is simply better for wellbeing to go with the flow of your authentic inner self. Knowing your limits is a key element of self-care.

Before going to Berlin, I had been fully attentive to the challenging stories shared within the ITSP, stories inclusive of those of Liberians, Jews and Armenians. I assessed I had already covered much of what might be gained by visiting Auschwitz itself. So, I walked instead to *Die Neue Synagoge* where I spent some enriching hours imbibing positive elements of Jewish culture, and then visited *Art Center Berlin Friedrichstrasse* also within walking distance. The latter to my delight had the magnificently large, colourful exhibition of contemporary works by First Nations Australians titled *Traumzeit* (Dreamtime).[7]

I then enjoyed a relaxing walk along the River Spree. During my time in this city, I also visited the Berlin Cathedral Church/*Berliner Dom*, one of its weekend markets where a Native American band performed, the statues of *Amazon Zu Pferde* (Mounted Amazon attacked by a Panther) and *Löwenkämpfer* (The Lion Fighter) outside *Altes Museum* (Old Museum) on Museum Island. Much I met in this city attested to the resilience of survivors of inhumanity. This is what I needed to strongly be in touch with – especially after seeing displayed photos of the destruction WWII left behind. These brought to mind my father who only once referred to Dresden in my presence. When he did so, his voice dropped. He whispered the name of this city as if in prayer. Having read S J Norman's *Unspeakable* since and learned even more about Auschwitz, I know I made the right choice to avoid raw exposure to its elements at that particular time.[8] Upon my return to New York, I chose to accept and focus on an opportunity offered to attend the United Nations Permanent Forum on Indigenous Issues (UNPFII) as an observer.

The discipline of Practical Theology has the capacity and potential to contribute positively to the field being considered if the patriarchal model of supremacy within European-based cultural frameworks is challenged alongside options solely focusing on specializations. Without such a challenge, more damage will be done to the life fabric of cultural minorities. Breaking the model of assumed supremacy over different ways of encoding and sharing knowledges will enable a liberating paradigm to emerge through which the flow-on effects of any genuine reconciliation attempt between peoples who are different yet 'equal' can incarnate. The past will always rear its head in the ongoing practice of reconciliation until the triggering of institutionalised supremacy is fully dismantled. It will only respond and ultimately be neutralised by hearts that hear the depth of residual pain via practising 'attunement'.[9] From this kind of attunement, intercultural life-affirming synergy can grow.

Recovery

The 'longest journey' is a term that can be used to describe the process of healing from rabid colonisation.[10] This song describes a country whose First Peoples self-determining livelihoods have been savaged. However, as James Cornell voices, the land still contains within it an ancient mysterious capacity to spring life forth again.

TESSERAE KINNED

THE LONGEST JOURNEY

This can be a holocausted country
My vast and wondrous land
Eden turned Gehenna
Charred silhouette
And smoking sand ...
But she has a way within her,
An ancient mystery –
Of searing forth the life source
Where prisons seemed to be,
A mellow way of wizardry
Patient earth, gentle rain
And warming sun,
A flutter of a wagtail
What was in the beginning is again begun.

They seem a scapegoat people
Pain for others' gain
Shackled for our freedom
Fractured dreams as we grow sane.
Their healing world belittled
Fringed to call us home
In their land that's been our Exodus
The Righteous now hear them moan ...
But there is a way within them,
An ancient mystery –
Of searing forth the life source
Where prisons seemed to be.

So, hold what's torn and broken
Till your loving makes it whole,
Find what's been forsaken

And rebirth it with your soul,
And to this scavenging of the spirit
Your people's kindling fire start –
Bring the lightning in your eyes
And the passion of your heart.
Bring the lightning in your eyes
And the passion of your heart.

Lyrics: James Cornell
Music: Maria Rosa

Yawuru elder Patrick Dodson expressed a similar connection with promise: 'You see, after years of holocaust ... there is a certain genius not extinguished within us. [It's] not a genius in the sense of being highly intellectual, but in the sense of something special in us that needs to be nurtured and cultivated and brought more and more into the light.'[11]

Visitors from 'Country' Elsewhere

'When are those young ones coming?' members of a group of elders enquired. Over the space of a few months, one or other of them kept checking in with the community Advisor about the intended time of arrival of 'the young ones'. He began to wonder what made this visiting group so distinctive and of such intense interest to the elders. They had not monitored any other visiting group's movements so closely.

After fifty years of minimal contact with the mainstream, the community members' vision for the tourism project revolved around appropriate cultural exchange with outsiders. They had articulated to each other and the community Advisor their aspiration of helping outsiders gain insight into their dynamic way of being, processed over thousands of years.

Before 'the young ones' came, a considerable number of pilot runs with tourists had occurred. The visitors entered 'country' via coach or Oka All-Terrain vehicles. Local community guides and translators escorted them to appropriate places of cultural significance. They met community members in such 'country' to safeguard the latter's privacy. Community members did not wish their living conditions to be photographed. Rather they wished to be encountered as 'a people'. A community barbecue, the viewing of performances and other artworks preceded an overnight stay by the tourists at a specially prepared, carefully chosen site.

Finally, the day came when a group of young people from a Melbourne high school appeared. This group's demeanour impressed me. Its leaders informed us that all had committed to doing a daily meditation practice together for weeks before the visit. I sensed they had created a resting space of open stillness, an intentional receptivity capable of absorbing whatever the elders and other guides might share. The delight on the faces of the elders grew as the tour itinerary unfolded and substantiated welcoming of their input emerged. Understanding engagement as being open to the flow of interaction and the relational rather than simply being a spectator tourist allowed deep mutual respect to be communicated.

When darkness fell, the elders performed two presentations of dance, drama and song never before shown to 'outsiders'. The elders too had been practising and preparing for weeks. The first performance addressed the arrival of other Australians in their country and linked it to a previously existing traditional story. The second presentation related to the fact that a dancer's sister had died. As the women dancers entered the red dust 'stage' and spread out, one followed close behind the bereaved. Sensing someone near, the bereaved sister would look around but the other dancer, anticipating this, would move deftly out of range of her peripheral vision. The dance thus progressed with moments of humour as slowly a poignant sense of someone missing forever from visibility emerged. Using no English, the dance troupe conveyed a felt sense of deep loss, a desire for a reunion continually denied, waves of heart-rending grief, resolution, acceptance and a new integration.

Stunned by witnessing such an unexpected theme dramatised so powerfully, the onlookers let the power of the performance remain suspended in the air when it finished. Then they burst into thunderous applause. In a language unknown to the audience, song had accompanied the whole performance carrying a message of experienced pain and dawning realisations. The display of appreciation and respect for the elders shown by the Melbourne 'young ones' inspired young people from the community to join their elders in song and dance for the rest of that evening. This phenomenon had not happened for a considerable number of years. You may wish to further examine the text *Melodies of Mourning* which comprehensively attends to the place of emotions and how these may transcend cultural differences.[12]

Courage, Song and Loss

Another example of song carrying the grieving process emerged in our family after my mother died. My father created a ritual from his sense of loss and emptiness. Upon awakening in the morning to realise my mother had permanently gone from his bed, his home and his life, he gradually reoriented his life through the prism of a song he felt closely expressed his feelings. He'd sing this vintage song from his own culture thus regularly saying good morning to sadness in his native language. In essence, he extended a greeting to a sadness whose potential depths he had not previously plumbed. He experienced sadness itself as a new companion vying to take my mother's place in his heart. The song spoke of yellow leaves as seeming to now be crying and the murmur of plane trees asking: 'Where is she?' The road he and his unwelcomed companion now shared is named as the same well-worn one along which he had intimately known happiness.

A time of sudden loss led me to write 'Black December'. In grappling with my father-in-law's death – also a sudden one, my husband and I wrote a song together about what we experienced as an unexpected change of season in our lives. It is my experience that music can truly act as an alchemist to accompany the acceptance of grief and embodiment of remembrance. The powerful combination of song with dance and drama can be transformative for the telling of meaning-making stories. This has been underlined by the Spanish Conquistadors' reputed cutting off of the feet belonging to members of First Nations in some places they conquered so they could no longer dance.[13] Perhaps we may be correct in saying that, in the absence of expressive arts involving the whole body, we may be at risk of becoming crippled in facing existing and future crises. Movement can minimise their more lasting effects. Conquering freedom to bodily process experiences, birth creativity and newness by members of a collective may appear to be one of the most damaging colonisations of all. We have come to learn from specialists dealing with trauma that individual bodies store and remember wounds not allowed into the light.

'Meeting the Waylo'

In her text *Meeting the Waylo*, Tiffany Shellam introduces us to *Ngungar* intermediaries who accompanied expeditions to map Australia's northwestern coastline. She reveals they 'mediated the strangeness of their own in-betweenness' via song.[14] In this way, they 'countered the cultural and environmental foreignness they experienced while exploring with Europeans in unknown Aboriginal territory, as well as the process of preserving their stories'.[15] The author explores the memory devices of Migeo and his mediating techniques through song so that he too – like the explorers – could inform his people on his return of happenings on the expedition. 'In an attempt to avoid the rubric of an explorer's journal', Shellam's text is not chronological.[16] She reminds us of the danger of which the human geographer Miles Ogborn has warned: 'putting too much emphasis on the power of the official written record. There are too many counter-archives and alternative archives for that to be an adequate account of the relationships between knowledge and power.'[17] Let us, therefore, continue searching for and attending to elements within which songs are written.

James Cornell and canine friend

CHAPTER 9

INTERDEPENDENTLY 'KINNED'

EULOGY FOR SISTER AGATHA

1. *Her voice is still like music about Wadeye*
   Her joyfulness still lingers amidst the trees
   For she will be remembered till the tide
   Stops muttering moments on the mangrove shore.

2. *She walked forth as a girl from clan places*
   And hers was the longest journey of them all.
   She brought her Dreaming from the Heart of Christ
   To those with fading hope and weary eyes.

3. *Agatha of Wadeye, you are loved*
   And from our lives and heart you have never walked away.
   Agatha of Wadeye, you are loved
   And from our lives and heart you have never walked away.

   Lyrics: Rod Cameron, June 1991
   Music: Maria Rosa

Rod had met Sister Agatha – as had I – and spent some time with her. Upon receiving the news of her death, he wrote a poem which I have adapted to create the above song. Sister Agatha came from the area whose centralised service centre is now called *Wadeye* (pronounced wod-air-yer).[1] Years ago, some called this place Port Keats or affectionately by the nickname 'PK'. In the past, twenty clan groups who spoke different languages resided in the area. In August 2003, the first *Thamarrur* Regional Council came into existence comprised of two representatives from each clan. The name *Thamarrur* is a symbol of the ancestors' relevance to 'the building blocks for the future'. Before that, *Kardu Numida* (translated as 'one people') Council existed since 1978. The people self-identify as *Wangka*, *Lirrga* and *Tjanpa*.[2] The traditional owners of the land where *Wadeye* is situated are the *Kardu Yek Diminin*. Until after the arrest and trial of the resistance fighter Nemarluk, the people of the area had limited, mutually beneficial contact with non-indigenous people. Catholic missionaries came to the area at the request of the government in 1934.[3]

During WWII, the people in the vicinity had dealings with the Australian Army. The links forged then came to the fore one time when we heard helicopters arriving on the airstrip not far from our classroom. In a heartbeat, all my students spontaneously evacuated and ran to enthusiastically greet landing defence personnel like heroes. The soldiers seemed startled at such a welcome, some even embarrassed. In Aboriginal English, we can describe the latter reaction as having 'shame'. After the use of troops in 'The Intervention', I do not know if a similar response to the landing of soldiers in this largest of NT First Nations communities would occur now. The Army itself may not be held responsible, however, for an essentially Federal Government directive to proceed with 'The Intervention'. Previously mentioned Dr Lowitja Lois O'Donoghue Smart, AC, CBE, DSG (of *Yankunyjatjara* and Irish heritage who has made a most significant contribution to Australian life) opposed 'The Intervention'. She said 'stripping people of control is not the answer: 'You can't just come over the top of people, you've got to talk to them.'[4]

Sister Agatha stands as a symbol of all the people at *Wadeye* who, over their lifetimes, strove to maintain a strong sense of identity while simultaneously working to bridge the gap between their traditional knowledge systems and those of the mainstream 'Anglo' Australian cultural institutions and their personnel. In many ways, the journey for the people of the area can truly be described as *'the longest journey of them all'*. Their endeavours to create meaningfully authentic lives and advocate for their heritage amidst the consequences of 'Year Zero' need to be heralded in many instances as remarkably resilient and immeasurably valiant.

I am ashamed to admit that, after being at *Wadeye* for a few months, I asked for a transfer! When I did so on a trip to Darwin, a wise person there encouraged me to give the connection one more chance. At the time, I did not adequately consider that only forty odd years had passed since the establishment of *Wadeye* itself. My confusion arose because no 'local' people seemed to engage me beyond the surface – that is what I missed. First Nations people I had worked with in other places had spoken much more *with* me sooner. They had been less reserved. As a young person, I felt the seeming lack of engagement keenly. My encourager said the 'PK' people would be 'watching you … working out what you are like'. Once I got a 'PK' friend, she said, I would have one for life. This came to pass and I am forever grateful I followed the advice given.

When one of the Indigenous teachers in my classroom there eventually and prophetically explained to me that the proposed way of managing the curriculum would not work, I breathed a sigh of relief. A great weight lifted off my shoulders. At last, someone here said what they really thought! I felt like flying some kind of flag at this revelation. After listening to the accompanying explanation, I knew the track to negotiate much better. Being in this community became another defining point in my understanding of in-between cultural spaces and blessedly informed it elsewhere via ongoing reflection.

I have an enormous respect for those people of Indigenous descent who led me to the insights I gained at *Wadeye*. From them, I learnt how unmet diversity affects contexts. The learnings have shaped my approach to Indigenous education ever since. They enabled me to increase the cultural safety of many other First Nations people to the degree that they successfully incarnated their articulated aspirations. What did I learn via defining moments at *Wadeye*? Never give up no matter how alien or alone you may feel or ill-equipped amid more traditionally-oriented people. Effective communication is possible – it needs time, being open-minded and a willingness to hear muted voices coming from within previously unmet differences. Yunkaporta clearly expresses the diversity protocol operating within interconnectedness: maintain individual differences with those similar to you, interact particularly with those dissimilar and be truly adaptive.[5]

Kin-dom versus Kingdom?

Kinship systems operate in a liberating way for all by creating a space that places everyone in a clear relationship with each other and the land. Some people of non-Indigenous descent avoid what they describe as 'getting caught up' in this way of organising and understanding life. Little do they know that often after they have been in a community for a locally specified time, an initiative or certain efforts they make may work across cultures simply because, unbeknownst to them, they have been placed and operate within the local kinship system. After you have been in a community for a length of time, a decision determined by the residents themselves may be made about where you fit kinship-wise. Someone is taking responsibility for you in certain culturally configured ways and you can socially exist within it, either formally or informally for yourself, as time passes.

How far we choose to consciously act within the local kinship system is individual. We cannot live a solo existence, however, and the kinship system formally recognises this interindividual reality. Even years later, far away from your assigned local kin, the realisation may dawn of what fitted where and we can only bow in gratitude for the understanding, compassion and courageous conversations experienced. A *malpa* (as mentioned earlier or other language equivalent) connected with your work may feature in your allocation within the kinship system. Therefore, in the negotiation of the concrete details associated with training partnerships in new communities, Keis and I initially sought a similar cultural broker willing to assist us. Thus, a 'kin-dom' enacted itself at times parallel to a hierarchical system/'kingdom'.

I remember the day in one community when an elder announced to me he was my 'father'. The revelation came when a concern of mine needed addressing. His announcement accompanied its prompt harmonious resolution and an invitation to approach him if any further issues of community concern arose. What a wonderful safety net for an 'outsider'! I noted he carried a small Collins English dictionary in his back pocket wherever he went and proved unafraid to use it. I like the following song whose music is composed by Ron Bopf OSA for it speaks of the gratuitous goodness we sometimes experience in the field where cultures meet. It often remains *'silent in long shadow time'* and can give us a *'glimpse at the eternal years'*. These lyrics speak into what Rod has highlighted of the psychologist Abraham Maslow's reference to 'moments of peak experience'; in such moments, one 'feels as one with humanity or with the world' and they are not reserved simply for great saints.[6]

ANGEL OF THE LAKE

Gentle angel of the lake,
Silent in long shadow time,
Moths in mist white pantomime,
From the walls of mystery break.
And from the night, a festive make.

Endow these pale moon thoughts of mine,
To fly where spirits live,
Loiter on the winds and give substance,
To the old designs,
For modern nomads at your shrine.

Stars are trembling in your tears,
Space is burning in your heart,
Spirit from your depths impart,
A glimpse at the eternal years.

It's true .... The gentle angel hears.

> *Lyrics: Rod Cameron*
> *Music: Ron Bopf*

Another Learning or Two

One way of broaching difficult topics of conversation which I learned in one traditionally-oriented, predominantly First Nations community is contained within statements like: 'I need to talk with you about something hard.' The person addressed in this way would, most likely, not respond immediately. Indeed, silence may ensue and the person moves on appearing to perhaps not have heard. If this should happen, do not panic! This is not rudeness. When the person is ready – perhaps even days later, you will be approached with something similar to: 'What is that hard thing you need to talk with me about?' or 'What is worrying you?' Allowing time after you have alerted the person you approached that you have a concern means they can prepare themselves mentally to have the kind of conversation required. This is a way of honouring the care many First Nations people take to avoid confronting or triggering exchanges. Thus, they culturally encourage productive dialogue.

'Many Australians are subconsciously socialised to avoid conversational silences or pauses.'[7] The one-second norm for silence is not shared by all sociolinguistic groups: Japanese people, Indigenous Americans, some Scandinavian and Australian Indigenous people are comfortable with longer conversational silences.[8] Extended periods of silence are a norm for them and allowing for these ensures the responder gives 'more considered and accurate' responses.[9]

Taking account of gratuitous concurrence is also most important. If a person feels under pressure to respond, they will cooperate with you in a default way to give the impression of agreement. Should you fill the silence and ask, 'Can we talk at 3 pm?' They may say 'yes' and then not turn up because they still feel pressured or unprepared. Even if they already know they are doing something else at 3 pm, they will not tell you. Culturally, they will work assiduously to avoid saying 'No' in any situation as they do not wish to cut off possibilities or run the risk of disappointing you by doing so. They will manage the situation by simply not appearing at 3 pm. This is a significant cultural difference requiring our ongoing awareness: 'Direct questioning is generally considered rude in Aboriginal culture and as a result, many, when confronted with it, may feel intimidated, "shame" (embarrassed) or uncomfortable. Unfortunately, from a mainstream cultural perspective, this fact has the propensity to be misinterpreted as a sign of guilt or evasiveness or untruthfulness.'[10]

'Nero's Fiddling While Rome Burns'

In 2003, the psychotherapist Dr Craig San Roque highlighted ruinous effects of interconnection: 'The tragedy in our antipodean country is quieter than that in Yugoslavia, or Sudan, or Timor; lethargic almost. Nevertheless, the havoc is conducted with predatory obliviousness to the personal human condition. Even in the benevolent offices of bureaucracy there is an irritable allowance for cultural annihilation, justified as abstract impartiality and rational economic necessity. We witness here the corruption and demise of the indigenous mind stuff. There is no obvious war here, just a slow demolition of a storehouse of creation.'[11] He elaborated: 'It seems that whoever it was who set fire to the library of Alexandria has been recommissioned to burn the library of Australia … A knowledge base has been lost of incalculable poetic and bioecological value.'[12]

In speaking to similar senseless destruction, Richard Trudgen questions: 'Is violence only violence when someone is physically hurt? Or is there a deeper, more destructive violence that destroys a people's soul?'[13] For him, institutionalised violence is the worst kind: 'It is subtle, almost hidden, wrapped in the ethnocentric paternalism of the dominant culture. Welfare and the dependency it creates is the worst form of violence. It has created a living hell.'[14] Notably, Barry Hill summarises paternalism thus: '(It) is, when all is said and done, the authority of false love: under the plan of doing good for people, it denies them their freedom.'[15] At times, the term 'tough love' can be used to cloak its appearance. While the past cannot be undone, it can be countered – not in a romantic way idealising 'the noble savage' – but, via dialogue that focuses on the kind of reciprocity encompassed by the term 'interculturation'.[16] This involves walking with knowledge bearers associated with 'major mythical masterpieces, dreaming tracks, songlines, geographical sites, locations of teaching, morality plays, mysteries, secrets, survival keys, geobiological maps, sexual instructions, fantasy, humour and derision'.[17] Befriending such knowledge can assist ensoulment and counter destructive violence.

WALK WHERE ANCIENTS WALKED

Chorus:

Walk in this sacred land,
Walk where Ancients walked.
Walk in this sacred land,
Walk where Ancients walked.

1. *Learn about this sacred land,*
   Move in its Great Mystery.
   Walk in this sacred land,
   Walk where Ancients walked.

Chorus

2. *Open to the moods of this ancient land,*
   Become a child of The Universe,

> *Commune with this land.*
> *Carry a stigmata of light,*
> *Walk where Ancients walked.*
> *Walk where Ancients walked. Walk.*
>
> *Chorus*

3. *Beyond the Dreaming in this land*
   Is a yearning burning love.
   Every blade of grass is blessed,
   Every trembling leaf caressed.
   Every leaf of every tree is blessed.
   We are loved. We are loved. Carry a stigmata of light
   Walk where Ancients walked. Walk where Ancients walked, walk.

   Chorus

Lyrics: Rod Cameron, 16 March 1994
Music: Maria Rosa

A Vehicle of Structural Disempowerment

At the Arena Forum in 2012, the *Arrernte Alyawarra* elder Rosalie Kunoth-Monks recalled feeling like an outsider in her own country, 'out of sync with the mainstream' and 'clinging to the essence' of being. She elaborated on the impact of the last five years under 'The Intervention' given 'the tremendous trauma' her people have had to carry as part of their 'horrific journey'[18] …

> we live in terror of our languages, our ceremonies, and our land being taken off us right at this time in our history.

My recollection of the Intervention at my home community *Urapuntja*, which is commonly known as Utopia, was the day that soldiers in uniform, the police and public servants arrived and we were ushered up to the basketball stadium and we were all told that we are now under the Intervention. We don't have access to newspapers, a lot of us don't have access to television, a lot of us were going along our normal way, living at home, and just doing the ordinary everyday things but on that day when they landed it was incredible. We really thought we were going to be rounded up and taken because John Howard had made the statement and Mal Brough of course carried it out, that we were now under the Intervention.

… the greatest impact of the last five years of the Intervention has been on the mental and emotional health in the Aboriginal people of the Northern Territory. People have developed a very deep sense of insecurity that undermines their feelings of certainty and safety because the age-old social structures are being eroded as we sit in this room. People from remote communities and homelands are being forced to recognise their own vulnerability.[19]

Allostatic load on people's health needs further consideration in such contexts. Rosalie pointedly underlined that she was not 'the problem' in an ABC Q&A television program.[20]

'The Intervention' is ongoing. Structural changes made and misperceptions acted upon in 2007 have solidified. Some who have had no dealings with the communities affected still maintain any 'problems' are to be placed firmly at the feet of 'the Council' in each community. They may not realise the disruptive NTNER measures undertaken included immediate removal and disbanding of all the then Local Government Community Councils. Community Council assets were confiscated. All those who had previously undergone Local Government Governance and Administration training with Keis and I had nowhere to locally and formally exercise their competencies. Accusing disbanded local Councils of failure to act!? This reveals a lack of understanding of the complete form 'The Intervention' took. It has been assumed centralised Shire Councils subsequently formed and covering enormous distances are just as effective with a Government Business Manager on site. Is this true? Here is a concrete example of First Nations people doing training for growing self-governance existing within the flow between cultures and then, without consultation, the mainstream structures impacting their decision-making capacity and significant parts of their lives are summarily changed.

No opportunity for free, prior and informed consent was given. We may ask: Do mainstream actors put themselves in touch with sufficient contextual reference points, including such consent, before making judgements and acting from afar? Here is one perspective shared: 'We believe that this government is using child sexual abuse as the Trojan horse to resume total control of our lands … That's why the Prime Minister called it a national emergency. You know, because in the national interest, he can move on the Northern Territory land rights act. Right?'[21]

Much has been said and written about what occurred in the lead-up, execution and follow-up of 'The Intervention'. Moral philosopher Raimond Gaita critiques the agreement of Indigenous activist Noel Pearson and others of non-Indigenous descent with it while closely examining the concept of 'reconciliation'.[22] Essentially he points to the continuing need for the slower development of friendship with First Nations people amid the 'moral bludgeoning' many have experienced through 'The Intervention'.[23] Talk of rights and accompanying responsibilities are summed up thus: 'The Aborigines have no power worth speaking of. If their voices are to be heard, if they dare speak from their hearts seriously to challenge our assumptions, be they assumptions of the Right or the Left, then it will be because we – the non-Aboriginal population – will have been moved by the spirit of justice to listen.'[24]

'Walk where Ancients walked'

CHAPTER 10

STILLING TERROR OF LOSS

THE STILL

I have loved the fiery youth,
The molten golden joy of dawn
Splashed across the skies,
But yesterday to my surprise,
I saw the sun rise elsewhere,
In the heaven of your eyes.

Elsewhere, elsewhere, in the heaven of your eyes.

I have been stripped down,
Dismantled –
Each wish, hope, feel
And future of me.
Stolen –
Dismembered me! Stolen!
I've been in the Still, the Still,
I've been in the Still.

Yet I still love the fiery youth,
The molten, golden joy of dawn
Splashed across the skies,
And, yesterday, to my surprise,
I still saw the sun rise elsewhere,
In the heaven of your eyes.

The heaven, the heaven, the heaven of your eyes,
Heaven – eyes, heaven are your eyes.
Heaven – eyes, heaven are your eyes.

>   *Lyrics: James Cornell*
>   *Music: Maria Rosa*

The composition of the music for this song grew out of the experience of living with COVID-19. It laments loss. Management of this global pandemic without vaccines involved strong movement restrictions; isolation from acquaintances, friends and loved ones; avoidance of physical touch without protective equipment; social distancing while engaging in essential tasks; mandatory wearing of masks and sanitising; deep cleaning; reliance on social platforms such as Zoom for connection and a sense of loss of freedom amplified by great uncertainty for everyone. Fearing the loss of repositories of wisdom, First Nations peoples in the pandemic's first year formed ARKS to safeguard their elders.

Agreeing to the discipline of being comparatively still – stilling previously standard/normal ways of interacting – has demanded intention, attention and strong commitment. In the Australian state of Victoria, the ensuing declaration of a State of Emergency followed years of drought and horrific summer bushfires in East Gippsland. Folks in Aged Care in Melbourne died separated from significant others. Like elsewhere in the world, the burial of COVID-19 victims had to proceed without the strengthening comfort granted by friends in more standard interpersonal farewells.

Amid the stripping down such discipline required, the basics of shelter, food, drink and human connection beyond mere transactions emerged anew as paramount for everyone. The premise of the 'mateship' code – caring for others' needs alongside our own in times of trouble – proved to be a safety net vital to survival and quality of life. It thankfully largely held and prompted heartfelt gratitude from many. 'Seeing' the humanity of others has proven to be both needed and redemptive. It has brought the possibility of confirming personal and communal acknowledgement, a recognition of common humanity. Indeed, the social psychologist Hugh MacKay noted an increase in kindness towards one another, what he called an outpouring of love.[1]

The image of daybreak in this song represents life-giving, insightful movement and celebrates the promise of youthful hope in our hearts for a kinder society – free of the contempt which can be directed towards those who do not easily align with powerful views, who are different. Within this promise, we can catch glimpses of the meaning within Desmond Tutu's words: 'Hope is being able to see that there is light despite the darkness.'[2] Such transformative light can dispel the darkness of illness, fear of health system collapse, loss, grief, job uncertainty, the threat to life, frustrating ongoing lockdowns and dissolution of much-anticipated plans. For First Nations people, the terror of annihilation needs to be transformed by such light. Accessibility to 'country' is a critical mainstay of their maintenance of wellbeing. In writing the following song, some of Rod's poetic words naming humanity as his 'country' inspired me.

YOU ARE MY COUNTRY

You are breathing new life into my being,
Breathing new life into my song.
Calling me close, close to your campfire
Softly singing a song, a song of love.

I am your country. I am your home! (Repeat)

O dearest land, O dearest friend, bring to life within me
What has been dead, dead for years.
Let me stand, in your conscious love,
So, I can let go all of my fears.

You are my country, you are my home (Repeat)

I hear your singing in the wind,
Feel your gentle touch in the rain.
I hear your laughter in the sky,
Your song in the water flowing by.
Your friendliness healing, healing my pain
May we meet, meet again.

> *Lyrics: Rod Cameron, Maria Rosa*
> *Music: Maria Rosa*

Unfortunately, some people simply place the First Nations understanding of 'country' – as well as 'Dreamtime' – in an abstract realm of imagination, into unearthed representation. However, as Deborah Bird Rose asserts, the definition of 'country' starts with the idea that, using Levinas' term, it is a nourishing terrain.[3] 'Country is a place that gives and receives life. … it is lived in and lived with.'[4] It is connected with heart – not just mind, existing 'both in and through time'.[5] It is 'synonymous with life'.[6] Sometimes, a person of non-Indigenous descent like Deborah Bird Rose, after considerable, disciplined research, can act as an intermediary in describing concepts others of non-Indigenous descent need to grasp. In her work *Nourishing Terrains*, she contributes to building a bridge of understanding about Australian First Nations meaningfully foundational 'country'.

> Country in Aboriginal English is not only a common noun but also a proper noun. People talk about country in the same way they would talk about a person: they speak to country, sing to country, visit country, worry about country, feel sorry for country and long for country. People say that country knows, hears, smells, takes notice, takes care, is sorry or happy. Country is not a generalised or undifferentiated type of place ... country is a living entity with a yesterday, today and tomorrow, with a consciousness, and a will toward life. Because of this richness, country is home and peace; nourishment for body, mind and spirit; heart's ease.[7]

Doris Stuart Kngwarreye points out: 'Apmereke-artweye – belonging to country – I don't own it, that country owns me, and that's what I stick to. I'm not a traditional owner – I don't own anything; the country owns me. And I have to do what the country needs to keep it strong.'[8] Other First Nations people also speak of their ongoing connection to 'country': 'Anangu [Aboriginal people] ... grew up on this land, going up and down, walking and on camels. We belong to the Finke and Palmer [rivers]. ... we are not moving from there. That's our land. ... We are still there nyinanyi ngurangka [staying at home].'[9] 'We cannot leave our country for the white people, for the government. We are government too, Anangu government. We were born on this ground, our birthplace. ... We can't leave our country.'[10]

I first began to get a sense of the meaning of 'country' when I accepted an invitation to travel some distance to attend a First Nations traditional dance get-together in the Kimberley region. The body painting and other materials used enhanced a vibrant display of many interconnecting elements. Only a handful of non-Indigenous people attended. I found myself in awe. The dancing accompanied by singing in the local people's language remains strongly visible in my mind's eye. There I met my first anthropologist – not that I understood then what these professionals do. Now though, I can understand why one person said to me that, if he had known what he now knew, he would have studied anthropology alongside theology. I am glad I subsequently did. It has trained me to observe with disciplined reservation.[11]

First Nations people, both adults and children, asking me 'Where is your country?' rather than first asking for my name intrigued me many years ago. I did not know then how this question led into the schema from which they operated.[12] Now, I know this question is the form a cultural introduction takes. 'Country' is the starting point of our life so knowing it makes perfect sense from a First Nations perspective. Understanding the meaning of 'country', we can give some visibility to how First Nations peoples know themselves to be, to exist within the singing horizons of a broader cosmos. The identifier of our 'country' is not simply a cognitive one – it involves a whole way of being, inclusive of soul. Looking to/after 'country' is an exercise in dynamic ensoulment.

Hence my use of the word 'land' (inspired by Rod, Aborigines and Torres Strait Islanders) in the songs includes the whole of the environing world: the seas, the ground which extends in all directions around us on the mainland and surrounding islands, the earth's atmosphere, the stars and beyond. In essence, this 'land' inclusive of its flora and fauna, acted and continues to act as a container for meaning, identity and much more. When speaking of his *jababa* (big brother), John Bradley who we noted earlier is not of Australian Aboriginal or Torres Strait Islander descent wrote that his *jababa* quietly and with great dignity taught him that the Law (with a capital 'L') travels through the sea and from island to island.[13] In the Gulf of Carpentaria land, this is signposted via the word *kujika*. This word speaks of 'a *Yanyuwa* way of knowing which, by singing, lifts and holds and animates both country and kin'.[14]

Increasingly within Australian society, perspectives of Aborigines and Torres Strait Islanders revealing alternate worldviews are being recognised as valid by Christians and others. The implications of such realities are slowly being addressed and embraced by both secular and religious mainstream institutions as mutual understanding grows. Can we hold open the space of potentialities where cultures meet long enough to allow those processes capable of yielding mutually desirable, sustainable results to take effect? How can localised agreement grow in the face of the structural disempowerment which has occurred? Can trust lost through 'The Intervention' grow back? The step of discerning an outcomes-oriented co-agency between local Indigenous peoples' marginalised viewpoints and those of others still needs recognition, support and strengthening.

Cultures in Counterpoint

Hugh MacKay reminds us: 'Harmony is not all sweetness and light – try Beethoven in full cry, or Shostakovich. JS Bach's fugues, like the best of jazz improvisations, demonstrate how different "voices" can appear to go off in different directions while still contributing to the ultimate harmony of a piece. Apparent dissonances resolve themselves.'[15] Indeed, a long past lively exchange between an elder and Keis found the elder asserting: 'I am a fighter!' To which Keis replied, 'And I am a lover!' The elder's wife then said, '*You two Christian men fightin' – you should be ashamed of yourselves!*' All somehow in the process got resolved carefully and amicably.

The octogenarian *Anangu* elder and renowned artist *Tjilpi Kunmanara Tjupuru* Burton died on 27 February 2017. (*Anangu* is a collective term used by the people speaking *Pitjantjatjara* and *Yankunytjatjara* to refer to themselves and *Tjilpi* is their generic term honouring a male elder.) Out of respect for the fact that he is now deceased, it is customary not to speak this elder's actual name and use *Kunmanara* in place of his/any person's name after this person has died.[16] In *Tjilpi* Burton's obituary for the national newspaper *The Australian*, Skye O'Meara wrote: 'To the many visitors who probed him with questions suggesting that his dedicated role within the church somehow diluted his commitment to culture, *Tjilpi* Burton would smile and answer, "It's the same thing".'[17]

Describing a commitment to his particular Aboriginal culture and the Christian church with the response: 'It's the same thing', *Tjilpi* Burton and his peers, however, still experienced a 'cultural invasion' against which they chose to protest artistically.[18] Deciding to enter the contemporary art world with a huge artistic protest required substantial bravery in his mid-sixties. His works point to a lack of a particular kind of respect experienced by his people and the presence of experienced aggression, sometimes subtle and sometimes not so subtle. Thus, many First Nations peoples hold on 'with grim determination to … cultural heritage while the outside world has increasingly sought domination over it'.[19]

Resistance is real. The existence of diverse cultural beings that essentially can work with each other to produce an ultimately harmonious counterpoint in outcomes is thus necessary. Some expressions of Christianity still are aggressive and fail to understand the expression of good already existent within First Nations cultures. The only way forward for such Christians is the obliteration of adherents' 'other' ways and removal of any hints of First Nations cultures. This fails to recognise where Christianity itself comes in a cultural package and the fact the person of Jesus Christ too grew and lived within a culture.

I composed music to the following words when past Australia Days came around with seeming insensitivity to Indigenous perspectives.

ANOTHER AUSTRALIA DAY

Another Australia Day has come our way
We think of our country
And with our hearts we pray.
We know that every nation has its Word
Do we have the courage to stand and be heard?

Can we face the shadows in our past?
Can we work for a peace that will last?
Can peace be our melody?
Justice our staff?
200 years or more of history is much less than a half.

Chorus:

We have a choice
We have a choice
We have a choice
We have a choice

Evolving our identity is a gradual process.
Knowing this is what we have to do,
We accept our power and strength of consciousness.

We can't absolutize our guilt or innocence.
Valuing ourselves is of essence.
Our way involves patient understanding
In the bush, in this land waiting.

Chorus

This demands a choice, a choice
This demands a choice, a choice

> *Lyrics: James Cornell, Maria Rosa*
> *Music: Maria Rosa*

Amid the complex layering of elements present in contexts of cultures impacting each other and acknowledging the existence of *Iutruwita*/Tasmania, James Cornell notes in the lyrics of this song that 'love' embodying respect for cultural differences that create 'cosmic confusion' for us can do much – even the seemingly impossible at times.[20]

STILLING TERROR OF LOSS

LOVE CAN SEE IN THE FOG

Chorus 1

Love can see round corners
Heavy as the hair of the dog
Love penetrates the darkness
Love can see in the fog.

1. *Table Cape Disappointment*
   But the Bluff stands out from the rainstorm
   Casts back the mist from the sea
   And in the midst of cosmic confusion
   Dumbly continues to be.

   Chorus 2:

   Love can see round corners
   Crooked as a cow-kicked dog
   Love penetrates the darkness
   Love can see in the fog.

2. *Spring follows the starkness of our winter*
   From bitter tears beloved – BELOVED!
   For the one who waits faithful on the mountain,
   With none but inner warning
   Night's dark grape
   Bursts to the wine of morning.

   Chorus 1

Lyrics: James Cornell
Music: Maria Rosa

Love in the field of cultures in counterpoint is expressed via gaining appropriate knowledge and taking due care in process. Showing compassion via interpathy can attract the accusation that you are 'a bleeding heart' – thus inferring insufficient exercise of 'tough love'. Such accusations may be arrived at without detailed contextual analysis. I suggest the following guidelines for gathering correct information: Refuse to use valuable energy triangulating. Go to the source of a presenting perspective. Converse with the actual people being impacted. Design structures and processes within which all affected have agency and a voice – not simply those culturally privileged or vocal. Silence itself may be rife with the wisdom of unspoken voices. Ideology may be identifiable via exclusion of dialogue and facts which raise further need for reflection, questioning and adjustment on the part of the dominant.

One way the mind of a non-Indigenous Christian may be assisted in discerning how to manage cultures in counterpoint is via the thoughtful, contextualising method of the theologian Bernard Lonergan. It dually considers both objective and subjective data which can seem a slow and painstaking process.[21] Yet, if we are to create paradigm shifts for greater sustainability and success of efforts, we need to search beyond merely transactional physically and culturally distant modes of connection and note: 'There may be more to it!' than initially thought.[22] Frank Fletcher MSC also researched the relevancy of Lonergan's work to engagement with our First Nations peoples.[23]

Inquisitive Desert Camel Project participants

AFTERWORD

'Unless there is a spiritual renaissance, the world will know no peace.'
'I am the vessel. The draft is God's. And God is the thirsty one.'

Dag Hammarskjöld[1]

This text is not prescriptive. It is itself a particular tessera in the grand mosaic of mystery called 'creation'. The title *Tesserae Kinned* endeavours to speak to and capture the reality that we can all learn from each other, no matter our heritage, in this journey we call life. Our journey is not made solo. It moves forward in what the Buddhist monk Thich Nhãt Hanh has called 'interbeing' – the interconnection of all things.[2] No-one holds absolute Truth. As James Cornell expresses succinctly, 'Truth will only speak clearly once we, together, continuously allow and hold space for it to reveal itself.'[3] While speaking about what we have experienced as truth, we need to avoid dictating the form Truth itself will take.

The same outward form can mean something different depending on the context. Hence the same outward expression can convey varying inner realities. Music for me contributes to holding spaces that allow for such storytelling. We need conversations capable of holding differences and interculturality.

Here Dag Hammarskjöld assists our conversational journeying:

> To have humility is to experience reality, not in relation to ourselves but in its sacred independence. It is to see, judge and act from the point of rest in ourselves. Then, how much disappears, and all that remains falls into place.
>
> In the point of rest at the centre of our being, we encounter a world where all things are at rest in the same way. Then a tree becomes a mystery, a cloud a revelation, each man (or person *brackets mine*) a cosmos of whose riches we can only catch glimpses. The life of simplicity is simple but it opens to us a book in which we never get beyond the first syllable.[4]

A mentor to a considerable number of people, Dr Cyril Hally SSC advocated consideration of the above 'see, judge and act' mantra on many an occasion. He is the 1995 recipient in Australia of the Philia Prize for Vision and Initiative in Religious Work awarded by the World Conference of Religion and Peace. Opposed to absolutizing individual, solely subjective interpretations, he valued the impartiality of facts and worked to obtain greater objectivity about happenings. He focused on people as vessels able to be graced with evolving fullness of intent and purpose if they remain still and open to working through more than one perspective to establish facts. One of his mentees alluding to him as a 'holy irritant' said Father Hally, drew him aside 'to do theology as a great storyteller. He inspired me to read, research and study well.

AFTERWORD

He had a breadth of scholarship and compassion that come from a life lived in graced solidarity with the human condition of joy, hope, grief and anguish.'[5]

Fr Hally wrote: 'Narrative is constitutive.'[6] He underlined that in some places European occupation 'resulted in genocide from disease and slaughter; in others, ethnocide from loss of land'.[7] Reflecting on Australia's bicentennial celebrations he asserted: 'The long-term effects of Anglo-Celtic colonisation on Indigenous people is a challenge to the conscience not only of citizens, and particularly the Christians of Australia but also of New Zealand, Canada and the United States – all Christian, democratic and wealthy societies.'[8] 'Precisely what can be done in the political, economic, educational and medical spheres … calls for the utmost imagination, creativity and wisdom that as a nation composed of both Aborigines and non-Aborigines, we can muster.'[9] Having personally experienced his mentorship, I hope you too continually meet people of his calibre who inspire you to participate in the continuing dance of life of which James Cornell speaks.[10]

I shall not forget Fr Hally honoured me by choosing to attend my doctoral graduation two weeks before he died. He greeted me with: 'About time Maria!' – a comment reflecting my time-consuming tendency to engage complexity and search even amid uncomfortable perspectives. Reaching the point of some kind of rest amid the complexities created by cultures meeting may be a task similar to that of the surfer getting beyond surging breakers to a point where the shore is visible from calmer waters. There reflexivity is possible. 'Swimmers' may survive by being given knowledge beforehand on managing the equivalent of any 'rip tides'. Conserving energy and having time to absorb happenings is crucial for self-care. Perhaps the term 'culture' itself may be alien in some particular contexts and helpfully replaced by 'ways of being'.

The 'see' in 'see, judge and act' requires the development of an inclusive 'double vision' to grasp that which can be in counterpoint with the mainstream. The 'judge' imperative needs to be suspended from mainstream perspectives long enough for the participatory voices of First Nations people to be properly heard. Perhaps 'discerning' is a useful term for grasping the paradox of emptiness which fullness of 'seeing' involves before the process of 'judging' leads to 'acting' in particular contexts where ways of being collide. To make sustainable differences, the imperative to 'act' must ultimately midwife collaboration, acknowledge nuanced realities and occur in tandem with articulated aspirations from First Nations peoples living within the particular contexts actually being impacted. In working out and negotiating 'acting', First Nations peoples can be our best friends and relationships of trust between us most productive.

Preconceived mainstream 'seeing' leading to the implementation of top-down solutions needs to disappear. To truly address all the relevant elements, the information provided by the traditions, cultures and experiences of First Nations people cannot be ignored, cherry-picked or erased. James Cornell's emphasis in his text on the need for a balanced genuine 'encounter' with the 'Absolute', 'self', 'other' and 'country' is noteworthy.

The author of *Warning* wrote: 'It has been suggested to me that John Howard was the first Australian prime minister who really understood how to handle a disaster, as his exemplary performances after both the Port Arthur Massacre and the Bali bombings of 2002 testify.'[11] Can we nevertheless still ask: Did his government ultimately fail the NT and its peoples in 2007 by intervening in their affairs the way it did? Were there other ways, less dramatic or distracting and more accurately informed, to address valid concerns? Was the one-size-fits-all blanket response to the contexts of seventy-three

AFTERWORD

prescribed remote communities uncomfortably paternalistic? Was the Federal Government suspension of the Commonwealth's own 1975 RDA a catalyst for a setback of monumental proportions in NT Indigenous peoples' relations with others?

Notably, the First Nations lawyer Larissa Behrendt points out that the NTNER 'designed over a forty-eight hour period in Canberra, with no consultation with people working at the coalface in the Northern Territory, and rolled out by people who were flown in was always going to be fraught'.[12] I recommend reading the review submitted by the Australian Human Rights Commission, statements by James Anaya (United Nations Special Rapporteur on Indigenous Rights), and the World Council of Churches Living Letters team.[13] We can find other perspectives too on the internet, for example, the exchange between Former NT Chief Minister Clare Martin and Professor Marcia Langton AO FASSA FTSE as chaired by Anglican Archbishop Philip Freier; also that of Marion Scrymgour, Former Indigenous Member of NT Legislative Assembly for eleven years. In my mind the agency of caring, committed First Nations men and women in their communities could have been structurally strengthened, listened to and mutually formulated outcomes supported instead. Harder work? Or less dramatic? Deeply searching questions remain.

I agree with those who maintain bipartisanship has not helped provide the necessary healthy scrutiny needed of 'The Intervention' over the years since.[14] And so, without such scrutiny, the *Stronger Futures* legislation in 2012 cemented the structural disempowerment of First Nations peoples characteristic of 'The Intervention'. Indeed, bipartisanship has effectively denied the Australian people any meaningful debate over the provisions of this legislation. While the *Stronger Futures* legislation is due for review in 2022, the flourishing of transformative praxis requires the contours of 'The Intervention' be critically examined in all its dimensions on a level playing field with First Nations voices of those immediately affected.

There is an extremely powerful, confronting poem by Samuel Wagan Watson of the *Birri-Gubba, Munanjali,* Germanic and Gaelic peoples. It is called 'Intervention Rouge'.[15] Though many may cringe at its prophetic words, it invites us to closely consider the way forward in re-imagining Australia with a comprehensive dissection of 'The Intervention' still front of mind. Can we together settle unfinished business with our First Peoples and dream into being a meaningful fullness of encounter incarnating the UN Declaration on the Rights of Indigenous Peoples (UNDRIP) to which Australia is a signatory?[16] I truly hope so.

Does the *Uluru Statement From the Heart* provide a gateway for enactment of these rights in a manner healing for First Nations? Whatever one may think of the UN itself as a current institution, it cannot be denied that a tremendous amount of work on the part of many people of Indigenous and other descent has shaped the content and import of the basic UNDRIP document. Such collectively attentive effort from many corners of the globe must not be wasted. Our Australian First Nations people offer us 'safe passage' and 'protection of our spiritual being' by welcoming us to 'country'.[17] May we reciprocally respond and ask: how can we transform moving forward locally and nationally in a way that challenges protective paternalism however intentionally benign?

> *The house without a window is hell;*
> *to make a window is the essence of true religion.*
> *Don't thrust your ax upon every thicket*
> *come, use your ax to cut open a window.*
>
> *Rumi*[18]

AFTERWORD

The government in Canberra had changed again, and now the intervention laws affecting his people were called Closing the Gap. It still meant that if you were an Aboriginal person living in a remote community on your traditional land, then you had less rights than other people in the country, and were forced to live under special laws that ruled over your life.

Alexis Wright[19]

Keis and Maria going to work one Red Nose Day

ABOUT THE AUTHOR

Born in *Naarm*/Melbourne, Australia, to parents who came from WWII-torn Europe and lived in North Fitzroy, Maria Rosa is the eldest of three siblings. The parents of her husband Keis (also born in *Naarm*) have European settler heritage too. For a significant part of their childhood, Maria and Keis lived on opposite sides of the Merri Creek.

Maria acknowledges the *Wurundjeri* of the *Kulin* Nation as the traditional custodians of the place of her birth. When she turned thirteen, her parents moved the family to Gippsland. They embraced this naturally beautiful part of the earth for the rest of their lives.

Attending school as a youngster and teenager with students from diverse European and Asian cultural backgrounds, Maria became aware of the need for and value of sustaining actively harmonious connections with people of different heritage.

Initially trained as a primary school teacher, she grew into secondary and tertiary education roles as well as other work. While embracing an invitation to travel interstate and enter remote Indigenous education, she became conscious of societally marginalised worlds for which she had not been fully prepared. A journey of conscientisation thus began bringing her in touch with beauty, *élan*, *esprit de corps*, much humour, and generosity which accompanied deep undercurrents of sorrow among the First Nations peoples she met. Much she realised had been ravaged via their meeting elements of cultures originating from overseas. Her labour involved much learning to make sense of the status quo and reasons for any barriers limiting participation at all levels by First Nations Australians.

During five years of observation, study, and immersion in the field of Indigenous affairs in various city, town, remote and very remote locations, Maria discovered the bridge-building power of song. It led her to musical composition and a serendipitous encounter with the published poetry of an Augustinian priest called Rod Cameron.

Maria accepted a bursary in the early '80s and thus completed a Diploma of Spirituality for Leadership. She then spent seven years as a secondary teacher in one of Sydney's strongly multicultural areas. Beginning singing lessons with Sister Mary Eleanor Macris RSC, Maria found her a keen supporter of her development as a singer and composer.

Then Maria worked as a counsellor and keyworker for adults with disabilities assisting them to articulate and achieve life goals. She met Enid McIlwraith with whom she recorded three programs for Radio Manly Warringah regarding the album called *Red Land Songs*.

With great excitement and anticipation, Maria and her husband Keis accepted an invitation to move to the desert hinterland. This meant the offer to have the songs played by an orchestra in Sydney could not be taken advantage of but valued correspondence with Enid continued. In the week before Christmas 1997, Enid wrote she was going to get in touch with Fr Rod Cameron who had overseen the recording of the album to tell him about her rescheduling of the three recorded programs for the next three weeks on the community radio.

The years of desert community immersion and work opened the door to Maria and Keis being hired as a professional team of itinerant lecturers. Both regularly travelled significant distances as requested to communities and homelands spread over the Northern Territory's vast expanses. They supported residents to meet their expressed aspirations as much as possible through the achievement of nationally accredited competencies. Their teamwork consistently focused on collaboratively developing models of best practice for engaging remote communities and homelands. Two-way patterns of interaction thus grew.

Maria subsequently spent time in the USA where she completed a placement among mainly *Ojibwe* (an *Anishinaabe*) people and an international trauma studies program. She became an observer at the United Nations Permanent Forum on Indigenous Issues. In the same year, the Federal Government led by Prime Minister John Howard propelled 'The Intervention' aka the Northern Territory National Emergency Response (NTNER) which swept through seventy-three prescribed NT communities. Through its all-encompassing 'special measures', Maria witnessed the complete dismantling of almost all structures within which the people in communities, homelands and outside agencies had meaningfully collaborated. She has since supported First Nations peoples' self-empowerment via her role as Theology and Ministry lecturer at the ecumenical *Nungalinya* College in the land of the *Larrkia* people, Darwin.

Awarded a professional doctorate in 2010 which concentrated on perspectives provided within intercultural and ethics studies, Maria continues to read extensively and passionately. On request, she has acted as a consultant, a mentor to remote community workers and composed commissioned music. Her qualifications include training in counselling, psychotherapy and advocacy, plus workplace training and assessment.

Maria has recorded more than fifty songs that build or reinforce understandings inclusive of the sacred in many contexts. The song lyrics can be used as conversation openers, witnesses to process, and catalysts for living with evolving questions. The *Red Land Songs* album released in 1986 has been used in various settings and has even been played in the mountains of Nepal!

Maria's interests include bushwalking, art, dancing, foreign language studies, and exploring links between health, development and human rights. They extend to the contexts of overseas Indigenous peoples – particularly in Oceania.

Another singing horizon

FURTHER ACKNOWLEDGEMENTS

I acknowledge the works of Rod Cameron OSA and composer Ron Bopf OSA in the intercultural space between First Nations people and other Australians; also, the permissions given by the Augustinians of the Province of Australasia to freely continue their promotion.

On 28 March 1983, Rod articulated our common aims:

1. To increase understanding between First Peoples and other Australians especially by using music and poetry as vehicles of communication
2. To explore 'The Dreamtime'
3. To communicate humanly significant experiences with Aborigines in cross-cultural contact
4. To embody aspirations of unity, reverence for uniqueness and a love of this land.

He consistently lived into this commonality of aims with great care, solidarity and refreshing humour. He is missed.

For genuinely thoughtful interest and ongoing commitment to the inspiration Rod Cameron gave many in the intercultural field of endeavour between First and other Australians, I wish to thank Dave Austin OSA and Peter Jones OSA (former and current Provincials of the Augustinians of the Province of Australasia). This intercultural field is often a contested one crucially connected with values central to building socially cohesive societies and nations.

James Cornell, another poet, author and songwriter also wholeheartedly and significantly engaged with the above aims. I wish to thank him most sincerely for his dedicated collaboration.

I especially wish to acknowledge the musicians and other creatives with whom I have worked – too many to list here. Particular mention needs to be made of those whose sound effects I have been able to use freely over the past years in creating the musical soundscapes uploaded to the website https://www.singinghorizonsrosa.com. There, sources of these sound effects and contributors to these versions of the songs are credited. On the website, you will find all the songs mentioned in this book.

For many years after the first release of the album *Red Land Songs* in 1986, my husband 'Keis' (a nickname he liked) invited me with some urgency to record my other musical creations. However, I delayed this task for a long time as work commitments pressed. The recordings on the above website have been completed long after the occasions for which I wrote them yet they would not be there without his insistence. In this text, all songs mentioned thus form centrepieces around which I share some of my journey of processing and learning. I wish to thank my beloved Keis for his ongoing encouragement, affirmation of my work and unstinting belief in me.

FURTHER ACKNOWLEDGEMENTS

Some of my compositions are still not recorded; some took longer to compose than others and to morph into their form as presented in the website albums. Rod Cameron and James Cornell, however, both invited me to continue my inclination to accompany their poem creations with music and work towards capturing more of the inexpressible in the power of song. James and Ron Bopf solely composed music for some of the songs I sing.

Some lyrics have not undergone any change from the poems. I used James' and Rod's words directly as written by them. In creating other lyrics, I weaved some of their words with my interpretations seeking to increase their accessibility for contexts in which I worked. At all times, I remain faithful to the overall intent from which these poets wrote. This text aims to present relevant background to some of the contexts which Rod, James and I personally and reflectively encountered. The music seeks to point to some nuanced realities greater than can be captured even by volumes of the written word.

Inspired by James Cornell, I decided to call this text *Tesserae Kinned* – a tessera being part of a mosaic of creation, all life forms. The 'kinned' aligns with his reference to Gabriel Marcel and Martin Buber's 'The Family of Being'.[1]

Together with the professional expertise of sound engineers Allan Black (formerly of Black Inc Recorders) and Brent Hodgkins (Warrior Records), a labour of love for the aims previously articulated by Rod has produced these songs as tesserae of soul and creativity. In this way, the songs too are 'kinned'. I also acknowledge the assistance of Al Craig (Black Inc Recorders) in the republishing of the album *Red Land Songs* in CD format for the first time and the staff of Implant Media for facilitating the production of the CDs for the album *Fire Wrapped in Stone*.

I acknowledge my singing teacher Sr Mary Eleanor Macris RSC who blew gently on the embers of my creativity. Apart from the songs I practised for her, she invited me to sing her my compositions saying my development 'fascinated' her. I still miss our times together. I also miss *Quandamooka* elder 'Aunty' Dr Joan Hendricks who used my songs in her bridge-building work and always supported my efforts in the same area.

Teresa and Allan Alexander have been instrumental in connecting me with the extensive work of Alice Duncan-Kemp, recording her unique story of interculturality written in and reflecting a different time. They and many others I know continue to constructively reflect upon and maintain interest in ongoing intercultural issues of importance to First Nations.

I especially cherish the friendship, courageous informative conversations with and accompaniment of feisty Barbara Higgins, Joanna Scheppingen Smith RN, Marie Chanel (Dawn Mokemoke McNicol) RNDM alongside connections with Heather McClymont RSM and Janet Connellan RSM at defining points in my journey.

I thank all those who have, over the years, encouraged me to write some of my experiences. You will know who you are. All my family, friends, colleagues and students are remembered here. Most particularly I am grateful to all those who have rejoiced and supported both Keis and myself as a professional team and 'kinned' in other ways, including through our shared interest in bushwalking, exploring this wondrous land and dancing. After his sudden death from congenital heart complications, I learned how grief itself deeply affirms the eternal. How can words do justice to all he meant to me and others? It would take too long to acknowledge all who have made a difference in both our lives, and who have stood in solidarity in various ways. Your life-affirming connections have embodied eternal grace.

FURTHER ACKNOWLEDGEMENTS

The recent Black Summer bushfires in East Gippsland brought the preciousness and fragility of life in all its forms to the fore. I wish to acknowledge all those who bore witness to the powers of prayer and being deeply held in the uncertainty of the present while endeavouring to absorb the effects of this catastrophe. I wish to acknowledge: the bravery and generosity of my neighbours; members of the Country Fire Authority; members of the Australian Defence Force; all volunteers including BlazeAid Inc, those from Fiji and elsewhere who have worked so hard to restore some sense of 'normality' in Eastern Victoria plus all involved in ongoing recovery efforts.

In reaching the goal of publication, I wish to acknowledge and wholeheartedly thank all the professional staff of Ultimate World Publishing – especially my editor Marinda Wilkinson. Many Australian First Nations people do not have a word for 'thank you' in their languages so, as some do, I say: 'Until we meet again.'

Leaving the past behind – a relic of terror

REFERENCES

ABC Religion and Ethics. 'God is a Wandjina.' Published Jun 28, 2021. https://www.abc.net.au/religion/watch/compass/wandjina-is-god/13403554

AIHW. 'Child Protection Australia 2013–14.' *Child Welfare Series, No 61*, 2015: Table 3.5.

Alaska Native Tribal Health Consortium. *Lateral Violence*. Anchorage, AK: Division of Community Health Services, 2021. https://www.iknowmine.org/topic/lateral-violence

Altman, J C and B H Hunter. *Monitoring 'Practical' Reconciliation: Evidence from the Reconciliation Debate, 1991–2001*. Canberra, ACT: Centre for Aboriginal Economic Policy Research, 2003.

Altman, Jon and Melinda Hinkson, eds. *Coercive Reconciliation: Stabilise, Normalise, Exist Aboriginal Australia*. North Carlton, Australia: Arena Publications Association, 2007.

Atkinson-Phillips, Alison. *Survivor Memorials: Remembering Trauma and Loss in Contemporary Australia*. Crawley: UWA Publishing, 2019.

Bain, Margaret. *White Men are Liars*. Darwin: Summer Institute of Linguistics, 2005.

Bain, Atwood and Fiona Magowan, eds. *Telling Stories: Indigenous History and Memory in Australia and New Zealand*. Melbourne: Allen and Unwin, 2001.

Behrendt, Larissa. 'Mabo: Ten Years On – The Legacy of Mabo: A Ten Year Assessment.' *Australian National University*, 2002.

Boochani, Behrouz. *No Friend But The Mountain: Writing From Manus Prison*. Sydney: Picador, Pan Macmillan Pty Ltd, Australia, 2018.

Bowden, Michael J. *Unbreakable Rock: Exploring the Mystery of Altyerre*. Churchill: Alella Books, 2020.

Bradley, John with *Yanyuwa* Families. *Singing Saltwater Country: Journey to the Songlines of Carpentaria*. Crows Nest: Allen & Unwin, 2010.

Bruce, Candice. *The Longing*. North Sydney: Vintage, 2012.

Burgess, Perry. *Who Walk Alone*. New York: Henry Holt and Company, 1940.

Cameron, Rod. *Alcheringa*: *The Australian experience of the Sacred*. Strathfield: St Pauls Publications, 1992.

Cameron, Rod. *A Look into the 'Eternal in the Now': Part 1 From Stranger to Welcomed One*. Video, Sept 7, 1988. https://www.singinghorizonsrosa.com/

Cameron, Rod. *A Look into the 'Eternal in the Now': Part 2 Life as Creative Journey*. Video, Sept 7, 1988. https://www.singinghorizonsrosa.com/

Cameron, Rod. *A Look into the 'Eternal in the Now': Part 3 Seeking the Good and Beautiful*. Video, Sept 7, 1988. https://www.singinghorizonsrosa.com

Cameron, Rod. *A Look into the 'Eternal in the Now': Part 4 Black Madonna*. Video, Sept 7, 1988. https://www.singinghorizonsrosa.com

Cameron, Rod. *A Look into the 'Eternal in the Now': Part 5 Where is your Country?* Video, Sept 7, 1988. https://www.singinghorizonsrosa.com

REFERENCES

Cameron, Rod. *A Look into the 'Eternal Now': Part 6 Actualizing Myth*. Video, Sept 7, 1988. https://www.singinghorizonsrosa.com

Cameron, Rod. *Karingal: A Search for Australian Spirituality*. Strathfield: St Pauls Publications, 1995.

Cameron, Rod. *Opala: A search for desert water*. Strathfield: St Paul's Publications, 1997.

Cameron, Rod. *The Red Land*. Sydney: The Augustinian Order in Australia, 1972.

Captain, Kylie. *Dream Big: Imagine the What If*. Diamond Creek: Ultimate World Publishing, 2021.

Caputo, J D. *Against Ethics: Contributions to a Poetics of Obligation with Constant Reference to Deconstruction*. Bloomington and Indianapolis: Indiana University Press, 1993.

Cilliers, Johann. 'Creating Space within the Dynamics of Interculturality: The Impact of Religious and Cultural Transformations in Post-Apartheid South Africa.' Paper presented at the *Secularization Theories, Religious Identities and Practical Theology Conference of the International Academy of Practical Theology*, Berlin, Mar 30 – Apr 4, 2007.

Collins, Ben. 'Being born in a remote leprosy institution just the beginning of life's challenges for health pioneer.' *ABC Kimberley*, Aug 28, 2018. https://www.abc.net.au/2018-08-28/health-pioneers-journey-from-leprosarium/10162018

Commission Submission in the Federal Court of Australia Queensland District Registry No QUD 300/2005. https://humanrights.gov.au/ourwork/legal/commission-submission-difficulties-facing-aboriginal-witnesses

Cornell, James. *Dark Diamond Dancing: a mosaic of encounter*. London: Athena Press, 2004.

Cox, Eva, 'The Intervention – Bad Policy and Bad Politics.' In Scott Rose and Anita Heiss, eds. *The Intervention: an anthology*, 195–211. Canberra: Concerned Australians, 2015.

Craddock, Robert, 'I'm going to chase some new dreams', *Herald Sun*, Mar 24, 2022:6.

Cunningham, Sophie. *Warning: The Story of Cyclone Tracy*. Melbourne: The Text Publishing Company, 2014.

Cunningham, Timaya, speaking on *Milimika* Circle featured on Essendon Football Club's Indigenous round guernsey design. In Liddle, Peter, 'Sir Doug Nicholls Indigenous round AFL guern(s[*sic*]) eys for 2020.' https://www.sbs.com.au/nitv/article/2020/08/20/sir-doug-nicholls-indigenous-round-afl-guernseys-2020

Dé Ishtar, Zohl. *Holding Yawulyu: White Culture and Black Women's Law*. North Melbourne: Spinifex Press, 2005.

Duncan-Kemp, Alice Monkton. *Our Channel Country*. Sydney: Angus and Robertson, 1961.

Duncan-Kemp, Alice Monkton. *Our Sandhill Country: Nature and Man in South-Western Queensland*. Sydney: Angus and Robertson, 1933.

Duncan-Kemp, Alice Monkton. *People of the Grey Wind: Life with a Stone Age People*. Oakley: D S Duncan-Kemp, 2005.

Duncan-Kemp, Alice Monkton. *Where Strange Gods Call*. Brisbane: W R Smith & Paterson, 1968.

Duncan-Kemp, Alice Monkton. *Where Strange Paths Go Down*. Brisbane: W R Smith & Paterson, 1964.

Dunleavy, Janine, compiler. *About Yarning Circles: A Guide for Participants*. Southern Cross University, 2013. https://www.scu.edu.au

Eades, Diana, FAHA, 'Taking evidence from Aboriginal Witnesses Speaking English: Some Sociolinguistic Considerations.' *Precedent*, 126, Jan/Feb, 2015:45-48. http://austlii.edu.au/journals

REFERENCES

Eppsteiner, Fred and Thich Nhãt Hanh. *Interbeing: Fourteen Guidelines for Engaged Buddhism.* Berkeley: California, Parallax Press, 1998.

Erskine, R G. 'Attunement and involvement: therapeutic responses to relational needs.' *International Journal of Psychotherapy*, Vol 3, No 3, 1998: http://counsellingvancouver/turningpointtherapy

Flanagan, Richard and Laura Tingle. *Podcast of Conversation*, The Sydney Writers' Festival, Jun 21, 2021, https://www.swf.org.au/stories/richard-flanagan-laura-tingle/

Fleming, Crystal M. *How To Be Less Stupid About Race: On Racism, White Supremacy and the Racial Divide.* Boston: Beacon Press, 2018.

Fletcher, Frank and Fabian Byers, ed. *Jesus and the Dreaming: Discovering an Australian Spirituality Through Aboriginal-Christian Dialogue.* Strathfield, St Pauls Publications: 2013.

Ford, D. *Theology: A Very Short Introduction.* London: Oxford University Press, 1999.

Gaita, Raimon, 'The Moral Force of Reconciliation.' In Altman, Jon and Melinda Hinkson, eds. *Coercive Reconciliation: Stabilise, Normalise, Exist Aboriginal Australia.* North Carlton, Australia: Arena Publications Association, 2007:295-306.

Garrick, Matt. *Writing in the Sand: the epic story of legendary band Yothu Yindi and how their song 'Treaty' gave voice to a movement.* Australia: Harper Collins Publishers, 2021.

Girard, René. *The Theatre of Envy: William Shakespeare.* Herefordshire and Surrey: Gracewing and Indigo Enterprises, 2000.

Goddard, Cliff, compiler. *Pitjantjatjara/Yankunytjatjara to English Dictionary.* 2nd ed. Alice Springs: Institute of Aboriginal Development, 1992.

Gordon, Deborah Christine, 'The Catholic Church and the Status of Aboriginal Women: Port Keats, 1935-1958.' PhD thesis, Charles Darwin University, 2004.

Grey, M. *Redeeming the Dream: Feminism, Redemption and Christian Tradition*. London: SPCK, 1989.

Haebich, Anna. *Dancing in Shadows: Histories of Nungar Performance*. Crawley: University of Western Australia Publishing, 2018.

Hally, Cyril. 'Bicentennial Reflections.' In *The Far East*, Vol 70, No 6. Columban Mission Society, Jul 1988:10-13.

Halpern Glick Maunsell Pty Ltd. *Kundat Djaru Layout Plan 1: Background Report (with 7 Amendments December 2007–May 2020)*. Perth: Western Australian Planning Commission, Oct 2003.

Hammarskyöld, Dag. *Markings*. New York: Ballantine Books, 1982.

Hansard, *Redress WA – Derby Leprosarium: Grievance*. Ms Josie Farrer and Mr Tony Simpson, ASSEMBLY – Thursday, Sept 19, 2013, p 4492a–4494a.

Hateley-Browne, Andrew. *Understanding Leprosy*. The Leprosy Mission Australia, Feb 8, 2016. https://www.leprosymission.org.au/2016/02/understanding-leprosy/

Helminski, Kabir, ed. *The Rumi Collection: An Anthology of Translations of Mevlāna Jalāluddin Rumi*. Translated by Helminski, Kabir and Camille Helminski. Boston, Massachusetts: Shambala Publications Inc, 2000.

Herzig, Maggie and Laura Chasin. *Fostering Dialogue Across Divides: A Nuts and Bolts Guide from the Public Conversations Project*. Watertown, MA: Public Conversations Project, 2006.

Hill, Barry. *Broken Song: TGH Strehlow and Aboriginal Possession*. Milson's Point: Random House Australia Pty Ltd, 2002.

Hughes, R. Interview of Lowitja titled 'Lois O'Donoghue,' *Australian Biography: Extraordinary Australians talk about their lives*, with prior interview by producer Frank Heimans, Film Australia, 1993–1994.

Kaggwa, Robert. 'Is Reconciliation the New Model of Mission? Reflections on the Rwandan Genocide and Conflicts in the Great

REFERENCES

Lakes Region of Africa.' In *The Edinburgh Review of Theology and Religion, Studies in World Christianity*, edited by Alistair Kee, 244–264, 9 Part 2. Edinburgh University Press, 2002.

Kaufman, G D. *In Face of Mystery: A Constructive Theology.* Cambridge, Mass: Harvard University Press, 1993.

Kaufman, G D. *Systematic Theology: A Historicist Perspective.* New York: Scribners, 1968.

Kunoth-Monks, Rosalie, *NT Intervention Forum*, Jun 7, 2012. https://youtu.be/lOhw-4KJPd0

Lifton, Robert Jay. *The Protean Self: Human Resilience in an Age of Fragmentation.* Chicago: The University of Chicago Press, 1993.

Lopez, Barry. *Horizon.* New York: Knopf Doubleday, 2019.

Macfarlane, Robert. 'Horizon by Barry Lopez review – magnificent on the natural world and furious too', Mar 14, 2019. https://www.theguardian.com/books/2019/mar/14/horizon-by-barry-lopez-review

MacKay, Hugh. Interview by Paul Barclay, 'Hugh MacKay on the "kindness revolution",' in *Big Ideas*, Jul 7, 2021; https://www.abc.net.au/radionational/programs/bigideas/hugh-mackay-on-the-kindness-revolution/13423434

MacKay, Hugh. *The Kindness Revolution: How we can restore hope, rebuild trust and inspire optimism.* Melbourne: Allen & Unwin, 2021.

Magowan, Fiona. *Melodies of Mourning: Music and Emotion in Northern Australia.* Crawley: University of Western Australia Press, 2007.

McAvoy, Tony, SC. 'Dr Charles Perkins Oration.' Presented at University of Sydney, 2021, https://youtu.be/A0ZnbRURAeY. Text of oration https://www.croakey.org/2021-dr-charles-perkins-oration-by-tony-mcavoy-sc/

McDonald, Heather. *Blood, Bones and Spirit: Aboriginal Christianity in an East Kimberley Town.* Carlton South: Melbourne University Press, 2001.

McFague, S. *Models of God: Theology for an Ecological, Nuclear Age*. London: SCM Press Ltd, 1987.

McFague, S. *The Body of God: An Ecological Theology*. Minneapolis: Fortress Press, 1993.

Men and Women of Central Australia and the Central Land Council. *Every Hill Got a Story: We Grew up in Country*. Edited by Marg Bowman. Richmond, Vic: Hardie Grant Books, 2015.

Metaxis, Eric. *Bonhoeffer Pastor, Martyr, Prophet, Spy: A Righteous Gentile vs The Third Reich*. Nashville, Tennessee: Thomas Nelson, 2010.

Miriam-Webster's Encyclopedia of Literature. Springfield, Massachusetts: Meriam-Webster. Incorporated, Publishers, 1995.

Moran, Mark. *Serious Whitefella Stuff: When solutions became the problem in Indigenous affairs*. Carlton: Melbourne University Publishing Ltd, 2016.

Mullett, Linda; Cheryl Mullett and Tim Leeson. 'An old place seen through new eyes'. In *Gippslandia*, Issue 21, Summer 2021:4.

Nakata, Martin N. *Disciplining the Savages, Savaging the Disciplines*. Canberra: Aboriginal Studies Press, 2007.

Nganbe, Tobias; Mathias Nemarluk, Aloysius Narjic and Theodora Nardu. 'The Past, Present and Future.' Presentation by the *Thamarrur* Regional Council Representatives at *Building Effective Governance Conference*, Jabiru, Northern Territory, Nov 5–7, 2003:1.

Norman, S J. 'Unspeakable.' In *Permafrost,* 115–135. St Lucia: University of Queensland Press, 2021.

Norris, Ray and Celia Norris. *Emu Dreaming: An Introduction to Australian Aboriginal Astronomy*. North Rocks: Emu Dreaming, 2009.

O'Meara, Skye. 'Desert mourns as Hector Tjupuru Burton, sage of Anangu, moves on.' *The Australian*, Mar 8, 2017. http://

REFERENCES

www.theaustralian.com.au/arts/visual-arts/desert-mourns-as-hector-tjupuru-burton-sage-of- anangu- moves-on/news-story/a3519e4cf2a9635113cd6b41558f6218

Panikkar, Raimon. *Cultural Disarmament: The Way to Peace.* Westminster: John Knox Press, 1995.

Pilger, John. *A Secret Country.* London: Vintage, 1992.

Power, Maria. 'An Exploration of the Nexus between Creation Spirituality and Aboriginal Spirituality.' Grad Dip in Theology thesis, Sydney College of Divinity, 1989.

Power, Maria. 'An Exploration of Practical Reconciliation.' DMinStuds thesis, Melbourne College of Divinity, 2009.

Power, Maria. 'Cultures in Counterpoint.' Presentation given at *Dreaming the Land: Practical Theologies in Resistance and Hope, International Academy of Practical Theology 2005 Conference,* Brisbane, Jun 26, 2005.

Power, Maria. 'Exploring Some Elements of an Inter-cultural Space.' In *Catalyst: Pastoral & Socio-Cultural Journal for Melanesia,* 42, no 1, 2012: 25-41.

Power, Maria. 'Exploring the Nexus – A Presentation of Some Points of Dialogue between Aboriginal and Creation Spiritualities.' Research MTh (Hons) thesis, Sydney College of Divinity, 1999.

Power, Maria. 'Practical Theology and Contextualising Research.' Paper presented at Association of Practical Theology in Oceania Conference, 2013. http://www.apto.asn.au/uploadedFiles/1367448387863-0279

Rainbow Spirit Elders. *Rainbow Spirit Theology: Towards an Australian Aboriginal Theology.* Revised ed. Adelaide: ATF Press, 2007.

Reynolds, Robyn, FDNSC. 'A Far Cry: Resounding Call to all Australians – Missionary Turned Around: Bound to be free.' *Charles Strong Trust Lecture*, Adelaide, Part 2, 2013.

Rintoul, Stuart. *Lowitja: The Authorised Biography of Lowitja O'Donoghue.* Crows Nest: Allen & Unwin, 2020.

Roberts, Janine. *From Massacres to Mining: The Colonisation of Aboriginal Australia.* London: CIMRA and War on Want, 1978.

Robson, Charmaine. 'Care and Control: The Catholic Religious and Australia's Twentieth-Century "Indigenous" Leprosaria 1937-1986.' PhD thesis, University of NSW, 2012.

Rong, Jiang. *Wolf Totem: There is much we can learn from the wolves.* Translated by Goldblatt, Howard. Camberwell, Victoria, Australia: Viking, Penguin Group, 2008.

Rose, Deborah Bird. *Nourishing Terrains: Australian Aboriginal Views of Landscape and Wilderness.* Canberra: Australian Heritage Commission, 1996.

Rose, Deborah and Anne Clarke. 'The Year Zero and the North Australian frontier.' In *Tracking Knowledge in North Australian Landscape.* Darwin: North Australia Research Unit, 1997.

Ruiz Wall, Deborah, OAM and Christine Choo. *Re-Imagining Australia: Voices of Indigenous Australians of Filipino descent.* Southport: Keeaira Press, 2016.

Ruether, R. *Gaia and God: An Ecofeminist Theology of Earth Healing.* London: SCM Press, 1991.

San Roque, Craig. 'A Rebirth of Tragedy.' In *Changing Places: Reimagining Australia,* by John Cameron, 159–169. Double Bay: Longueville Books, 2003.

Schillebeeckx, E. *Church: The Human Story of God.* London: SCM Press, 1990.

Scott, Rosie and Anita Heiss, eds. *The Intervention: an anthology.* Canberra: Concerned Australians, 2015.

Scott Peck, M. *The Different Drum: The creation of true community – the first step to world peace.* Melbourne: Rider, 1987.

Senior Secondary Assessment Board of South Australia. *Australia's Indigenous Languages.* Wayville, South Australia: Commonwealth of Australia, 1996.

REFERENCES

Shellam, Tiffany, *Meeting the Waylo: Aboriginal Encounters in the Archipelago*. Crawley: University of Western Australia Publishing, 2019.

Smith, Mike and Margo Neale, ed. 'The metaphysics of songlines.' In *Songlines: Tracking the Seven Sisters*. Canberra, National Museum Press, 2017: 216–219.

Smolinski, Henry; Paul Galloway and Justin Laycock. 'Pindan soils in the La Grange area, West Kimberley: land capability assessment for irrigated agriculture,' *Resource management technical report 396*. Perth: Department of Agriculture and Food, Western Australia, 2016.

Stafford, Megan, *Lenore's life on the land*, Jun 4, 2012. https://www.farmonline.com.au/story/3607082/lenores-life-on-the-land

Steering Committee for the Review of Government Service Provision. *Overcoming Indigenous Disadvantage Key Indicators: Overview*. Melbourne: Productivity Commission, 2011.

Steindl-Rast, David. 'Episode: The Monk and the Rabbi.' In *Any Given Moment, by The Unlearning Specialist, Link TVs Lunch with Bokara 2005*, Nov 6, 2014. https://schoolofmedia.com/2014

Steindl-Rast, David. 'How to be Grateful in Every Moment (But Not for Everything).' In *Onbeing* with Krista Tippett, Jan 21, 2016. https://onbeing.org/programs/david-steindl-rast-how-to-be-grateful-in-every-moment

Steinhauer, Yvette. 'A M Duncan-Kemp: Her life and work.' In *Journal of Australian Studies*, 25:67, 37-43, DOI:10.1080/14443050109387637

Swain, Tony. *A Place for Strangers: towards a history of Australian Aboriginal being*. Melbourne: Cambridge University Press, 1993.

Tonkinson, Robert. *The Jigalong Mob: Aboriginal Victors of the Desert Crusade*. San Francisco: Benjamin-Cummings Publishing Company, 1974.

Trudgen, Richard. *Why Warriors Lie Down and Die: towards an understanding of why Aboriginal people of Arnhem Land face the greatest crisis in health and education since European contact, Djambat Mala.* Darwin: Aboriginal Resource and Development Services Inc, 2000.

Tutu, Desmond Mpilo and John Allen, eds. *God Is Not a Christian: Speaking truth in times of crisis.* Sydney: Rider, 2011.

Woorunmurra, Banjo and Howard Petersen. *Jandamarra and the Bunuba Resistance: a true story.* Broome: Magabala Books, 2011.

Wright, Alexis, 'Be Careful about Playing with the Path of Least Resistance.' In Scott, Rosie and Anita Heiss, eds. *The Intervention: an anthology.* Canberra: Concerned Australians, 2015: 232–244.

Yunkaporta, Tyson. *Sand Talk: How Indigenous Thinking Can Save The World.* Melbourne: The Text Publishing Company, 2019.

NOTES

All songs may be listened to via
www.singinghorizonsrosa.com in indicated albums
(Abbreviations below)

Red Land Songs (RLS)
Fire Wrapped in Stone (FWS)
Wildfire Spun (WS)
Overheard by the Heart (OH)
Little Deep Wells (LDW)

1. Cameron, *Karingal*, 56.
2. Example of name change.
3. Please note that, to protect their privacy, none of the First People who grew me up in their ways are identified.

PROLOGUE

1. Mathnawi IV, 2619–2622 in Helminski, *The Rumi Collection*, 179.
2. Cameron, 1991.
3. Macfarlane, 'Horizon by', 2019.
4. The refugee advocate Behrouz Boochani refers to 'the principle of The Kyriarchal System' in his book *No Friend But*, 124.
5. Last 2 lines from the song: 'When the Wattles Bloom', Dec 29, 1998.
6. See https://www.abc.net.au/news/2020-6-18/drug-driving-laws-cannabis-nsw-unfair-magistrate-david-heilpern/12361312
7. Quoting Ginetta Sagan.
8. Quoting Dr. Martin Luther King Jr.
9. For example, Reynolds, *A Far Cry*, 5.
10. 'Level' is a word used by some people of Indigenous descent I met to describe something that is fair even amid differences, honest, balanced, and open to growth from the inside in all parties.
11. Macfarlane, 'Horizon by', 2019.

INTRODUCTION - SINGING INTO THE WIND

'Black December' (OH)
'Ode to Youth: The Old and The New' (FWS)

1. For text of *Uluru Statement from The Heart* see https://ulurustatement.org/the-statement.

2. Harold Thomas, a *Luritja* man from Central Australia and member of the Stolen Generations, created this flag in 1970. It was first raised on Jul 9, 1971 and in 1995 recognised as an official 'Flag of Australia' under *The Flags Act 1953.* https://aiatsis.gov.au/explore/aboriginal-flag
3. Period drama set in Canada and released in 1989 by Amazing Spirits Production Ltd, it tells the story of *Komi* taken to be 'civilized'; can be viewed at https://youtu.be/Os5KqErc7XY
4. Oct 2004. *Tapu* can be translated as holiness; *Karakia* as worship and *wairua* as spirit. Source: 'Kiwis' involved in ceremony.
5. See https://iknowmine.org/topic/lateral-violence Last updated May 2021; citing *Native American Women's Association of Canada. Aboriginal Lateral Violence: What is It? Fact Sheet on Aboriginal Lateral Violence.* https://www.nwac.ca/wpcontent/uploads/content/2015/05/2011
6. Senior Secondary Assessment Board of South Australia, *Australia's Indigenous*, 72
7. Haebich, *Dancing in Shadows*, 5.
8. Yunkaporta, *Sand talk*, 224. The *Alpech* clan is from Western Cape York.
9. Panikkar, *Cultural Disarmament*, 34.
10. Deborah Ruiz Wall, interview by author, Sept 10, 2005.
11. Cunningham, *Warning*, 43.
12. Ibid, 62; drawing our attention to the content of Sansom, Basil, 'In the absence of vita as genre: the making of the Roy Kelly story'. In Bain and Magowan, eds., *Telling Stories: Indigenous*, 2001.
13. Ibid; citing Rose and Clarke, 1997.
14. Boochani, 124.
15. Asserted Oct 4, 2014 during presentation at Tabor College, Adelaide.
16. Cunningham, 11.

CHAPTER 1 - SINGING IN THE SUN

> 'I Walk by Night/Not Alone' (RLS)
> 'Rest – A Lullaby' (FWS)
> 'Angels in the Dust' (FWS)
> 'Red Land' (RLS)

1. Rod Cameron, transcript by author of his presentation at the Innisfail Concert, Jan 20, 1987.
2. Steering Committee for the Review of Government Service Provision, *Overcoming Indigenous*, 3.
3. The term *pindan* used in the Kimberley region of Western Australia describes red soil country. It comes 'from local indigenous language and applies to the soil and landscape, and to the associated Acacia-dominant vegetation' (Smolinski; Galloway and Laycock, *Resource Management*, 1).
4. Gordon, *The Catholic Church*, 15.

NOTES

5. Collins, 'Being born', 2018.
6. Extract from Hansard, Sept 19, 2013, p 4492a–4494a.
7. For a photo of this church and some of the story surrounding it plus how two communities developed side by side: *Djarindjin* and Lombadina. https://djarindjin.org.au/historical-story-lombadina-mission/
8. Bowern, 'Aboriginal Placenames 14. Naming Bardi Places', https://press-files.anu.edu/downloads/press/p17331/
9. https://www.migrationheritage.nsw.gov.au/exhibition/objectsthroughtime/bourketerra/
10. https://officeforwomen.sa.gov.au/womens-policy/125th-anniversary-of-suffrage/aboriginal-women-and-the-vote
11. Check with Aboriginal/Indigenous Literacy Foundations.
12. Goddard, *Pitjantjatjara/Yankunytjatjara*, 61.
13. https://www.osa.org.au/vocations/the-augustinians/
14. Norris and Norris, *Emu Dreaming*, 3.
15. Ibid.
16. Garrick, *Writing in the Sand*, 34.
17. Local First Nations people can give their names of areas covered by this city.
18. Norris and Norris, 6.
19. Communication Jan 15, 1989.
20. Check with local First Nations people for their names of areas covered by this city.
21. Power, *Exploring the Nexus*, 67-72.

CHAPTER 2 - SINGING SILENCE

> 'Alcheringa' (FWS)
> 'The Stream' (RLS)
> 'On the Darling/Red, Black and Gold' (RLS)
> 'Australia' (RLS)

1. Rod Cameron speaking at Innisfail concert, 1987.
2. Bowden, *Unbreakable Rock*, xvi.
3. Ibid, xvii.
4. Ibid, xv.
5. The term 'country' is land inclusive of the seas and skies to which First Peoples are connected in a complex way.
6. Diagram – Figure 8 in Power, *Exploring the Nexus*, 301.
7. Cornell, *Dark Diamond Dancing*, 173.
8. Smith, 'The metaphysics of songlines,' In Margo Neale, ed. 2017: 216–219.
9. Ibid, 219.
10. Ibid, 217.
11. Ibid, 218.
12. Discussed in Power, *An Exploration of the Nexus*, 'Introduction', 61-62.

13. Cornell, 137.
14. Ibid.
15. Ibid.
16. Behrendt, 'Mabo Ten Years On', 5.
17. Text of the *Commonwealth Racial Discrimination Act 1975* can be accessed via http://www.legislation.gov.au/Details/C2016C00089
18. https://humanrights.gov.au/our-work/suspension-and-reinstatement-rda-and-special-measures-nter
19. https://www.nma.gov.au/defining-moments/resources/aboriginal-land-rights-act
20. Fleming, *How to be less Stupid*, 200.
21. Moran, *Serious Whitefella Stuff*, 4, citing 2011 Census.
22. Ibid, 1.
23. Ibid, 2, citing article http://www.biomedcentral.com/1472-698X/7/9
24. Ibid, 6–7, citing from Hunter, B. 'Conspicuous Compassion and Wicked Problems: The Howard Government's National Emergency in Indigenous Affairs.' In *Agenda*, Vol 14, No 3, 2007, 35–51. http://www.aihw.gov.au/WorkArea/DownloadAsset.aspx?id=60129550859
25. Ibid, 4.
26. Ibid, 9.
27. Australian in my difference: Women and migration in Australia since 1945. 'Deborah Ruiz Wall, Philippines', *Australian Women's Archives Project, 2006.* http://www.womenaustralia.info/exhib/aimd/aimd-15.html
28. Ibid, 1.

CHAPTER 3 – CIRCA KING SOUND

'Boabab Tree'/'Tree Spirit' (RLS)
'Wandjina' (RLS)

1. Rod shared this at the Innisfail 1987 concert.
2. https://www.kimberleyland.com.au/things-to-do/prison-boabab-tree
3. https://www.abc.net.au/news/2017-03-23/derby-boab-prison-tree-a-myth/
4. See Woorunmurra and Petersen, *Jandamarra and the*, 2011.
5. Hateley-Browne, 'Understanding Leprosy', 2016.
6. Burgess, *Who Walk Alone.*
7. Check with *Larrakia* people for correct name(s) for areas in Darwin.
8. For more information, see Robson, *Care and Control*, 2012.
9. See ABC Religion and Ethics, *Compass*, Jul 2, 2021.
10. 'God is a Wandjina' broadcast Jul 4, 2021 on the *ABC Religion and Ethics Report*. Ibid.
11. Ibid, Narrator.
12. Ibid.
13. Ibid.
14. Ibid.

NOTES

CHAPTER 4 - WELCOMING PRESENCE

> 'La Grange'/'Dreamtime Music' (RLS)
> 'Riding into the Wind – For Teresa' (OH)
> 'When the Wattles Bloom' (FWS)

1. Augustinians Australia 150, 'A little girl who bridged gap of centuries.' *The Catholic Leader*, Aug 7, 1988.
2. Men and Women of Central Australia, *Every Hill*, 33.
3. Tonkinson, *The Jigalong Mob*, 614–615.
4. Power, *An Exploration of Practical*, 7, citing Cilliers, 'Creating Space Within', 1.
5. *Malpa* is a *Pitjantjatjara/Yankunytjatjara* word to describe someone acting in a companioning role. See Goddard, 60.
6. This is a 'Tinglish' (Thai-English) phrase used humorously.
7. See for example: Duncan-Kemp, *Our Sandhill Country*, 1933.
8. A 'Troopie' is the name colloquially given to a closed-in Toyota with seats running sideways behind the driver.
9. Halpern Glick Maunsell Pty Ltd, *Kundat-Djaru Layout*, Oct 2003, 1–4.
10. https://theconversation.com/oral-testimony-of-an-aboriginal-massacre-now-supported-by-scientific-evidence-85526
11. Stafford, *Lenore's life on,* 2012.
12. Ibid.
13. Ibid.
14. See https://www.bidyadanga.org.au/
15. Atkinson-Phillips, *Survivor Memorials*, 47; citing Batten, B and P Batten, 'Memorialising the Past: is there an "Aboriginal" way?' In *Public History Review*, Vol 15, 2008, 103.

CHAPTER 5 - 'STORYING'

> 'Brolga' (RLS)
> 'Our Tracker' (OH)
> 'Story' (OH)
> 'Will All the Campfires Fail?' (FWS)
> 'Prayer for Creation' (OH)

1. Girard, *A Theatre of Envy*, 2000.
2. See McAvoy, Tony, SC. *Dr Charles Perkins Oration*, 2021.
3. Cornell, 30.
4. See Power, *Exploring the Nexus*, 32; citing Swain, *A Place for*, 255.
5. I wrote a first version text for this section in one of the 2021 productions of a local community newsletter.
6. Yunkaporta, *Sand talk*, 170.
7. Dunleavy, *About Yarning Circles*.
8. Yunkaporta, 273.

9. CIBIS. 'Software supports Indigenous', Oct 13, 2015.
10. http://www.whywarriors.com.au
11. Q&A, Question 61, Q&A, https://youtu.be/vAvCBJrEvlo accessed Nov 17, 2021.
12. This term is used by the author Jiang Rong in his book *Wolf Totem* to assist in capturing differences in life approach between the nomads of the Inner Mongolian grasslands and members of the People's Republic focused on modernity and productivity. I have borrowed it as it helps us remember Australian First Nations broader, more holistic perspectives.
13. Ms Timaya Cunningham from Xavier Catholic College speaking of 2020 Essendon Football Club's Indigenous round guernsey design. See https://www.sbs.com.au/nitv/article/2020/08/20/sir-doug-nicholls-indigenous-round-afl-guernseys-2020
14. Senior Secondary Assessment Board of South Australia, 77–78.
15. Ibid, 78.
16. Ibid.
17. McDonald, *Blood, Bone and Spirit*, 192–193, with reference to Caputo, Kaufman, Schillebeeckx, Grey, McFague and Ruether. The author further explains: 'The concept of salvation is currently being dehellenised. In the Hellenistic schema, humans are in exile from celestial plenitude. They seek salvation from the corporeal realm of evil and darkness in order to realise their true (celestial) being. However, Ford, in his *Introduction to Theology* equates salvation with health. This is a return to an archaic, locative concept of salvation' (216–217).
18. Ibid, 201.
19. See Bain, *White Men are Liars* for use of this metaphor; also shared personally in interview Dec 5, 2005.
20. 'Give us this day our daily bread' – Luke 11:3 from CPDV (Catholic Public Domain Version) Bible, published 2009; see http://www.sacredbible.org/catholic/NT-03_Luke.htm#11 (as at Nov 7, 2016).

CHAPTER 6 – 'NOT FAR FROM OODNADATTA'

'Black Madonna' (RLS)
'Paperbark Trees'/'At Camp' (RLS)

1. At Innisfail concert 1987.
2. Meriam-Webster's, 586.
3. Rintoul, *Lowitja: The Authorised Biography*, 144.
4. Ibid.
5. Ibid, 146.
6. Ibid.
7. Ibid.
8. Ibid; originally from O'Donoghue, Lowitja, 'Speech to the United Nations Association of Australia', Canberra, Sept 14, 1991.
9. Ibid, 147, cited from Hughes, R, Interview of Lowitja titled 'Lois O'Donoghue'.

NOTES

10. Ibid, 180–181.
11. Pugliese, Karen aka Pabàmàdiz. 'With the help of the Mounties, the priests piled the children into boats and floated away.' In *Canada's National Observer*, Jun 30, 2021. https://www.nationalobserver.com/2021/6/29/opinion/bury-myth-residential-schools-built-for-education
12. Ibid.
13. Dé Ishtar, *Holding Yawulyu*, xxiii.
14. Ibid, 189.

CHAPTER 7 – BEYOND 'TINSEL' BINARIES

> 'Fringe Dweller' (LDW)
> 'Kiata To Ki-in-Kumi' (FWS)
> 'Dancing Spirit' (OH)

1. Flanagan and Tingle, *Podcast of Conversation*, 2021.
2. Ibid.
3. Ibid.
4. Steindl-Rast, Jan 21, 2016.
5. Steindl-Rast, Nov 6, 2014.
6. Steindl-Rast, Jan 21, 2016.
7. For fuller description, see Bradley with *Yanyuwa* Families, *Singing Saltwater Country*, 27–28.
8. Ibid.
9. Ibid.
10. Ibid.
11. Captain, *Dream Big*, 74.
12. 'O'Donoghue, Lowitja (Lois) AC, CBE, AO', https://www.womenaustralia.info/leaders/blogs/WLE0354b.htm
    I recommend reading the story of Yothu Yindi in Garrick's epic story *Writing in the Sand* to gain further understanding of the context. Who originally used 'soothing of the dying pillow' is unclear for attribution. It is often used when describing the effects of the policy of 'protection'.

CHAPTER 8 – 'HARVEST HAPPINESS'

> 'Fireglow' (WS)
> 'The Longest Journey' (WS)

1. Cornell, 55.
2. Ibid.
3. Rainbow Spirit Elders, *Rainbow Spirit Theology*, vii.
4. Trudgen, *Why Warriors*, 197.
5. Ibid, 196.
6. Men and Women of Central Australia and Central Land Council, Foreword.

7. On Oct 9, 2021, one could still read a little of what the exhibition comprised at http://www.art-place-berlin.com/english/02pastprojects/07-australia.html
8. Norman, 'Unspeakable', in *Permafrost*, 115–135.
9. One definition of attunement 'is a kinesthetic and emotional sensing of others knowing their rhythm, affect and experience by metaphorically being in their skin, and going beyond empathy to create a two-person experience of unbroken feeling connectedness by providing a reciprocal affect and/or resonating response' – Erskine, 'Attunement and Involvement'.
10. Used by Rod Cameron too to describe the journey of Sr Agatha *Midaringi* FDNSC.
11. Power, *Exploring the Nexus*, 68; citing Pilger, *A Secret Country*, 66–67.
12. Magowan, 2007.
13. A former peer drew my attention to this fact. He had worked among people whose oral traditions spoke of such happenings. One incident of amputations of feet and hands occurred after the battle between the Acoma and Spaniards.
14. Shellam, Tiffany, *Meeting the Waylo*, 59.
15. Ibid.
16. Ibid, 16.
17. Ibid; citing Ogborn, M, 'Archives.' In *The Sage Handbook of Geographical Knowledge,* edited by Agnew and Livingstone, Thousand Oaks: Sage Publications, 2100:91.

CHAPTER 9 – INTERDEPENDENTLY 'KINNED'

'Eulogy for Sister Agatha' (LDW)
'Angel of the Lake' (RLS)
'Walk Where Ancients Walked' (FWS)

1. *Wadeye – Thamarrurr* Development Corporation See https://thamarrurr.org.au for more information
2. Welcome to Country – Thamarrurr Development Corporation thamarrurr.org.au
3. Ibid, 'Wadeye'.
4. Rintoul, 324; citing from source: Rintoul and Lunn, in *The Australian*, Jun 22, 2007:4.
5. Yukaporta, 266–273.
6. Excerpted from Cameron, Rod, 1995, by Bayly, Michael J. http://thewildreed.blogspot.com.au/2006/09/ Sept 25, 2006.
7. Eades, *Taking Evidence From*, 48.
8. Ibid, 4.7.
9. Commission Submission, No QUD 300/2005. https://humanrights.gov.au/ourwork/legal/commission-submission-difficulties-facing-aboriginal-witnesses
10. Ibid.

NOTES

11 San Roque, 'A Rebirth of Tragedy', 165–166.
12 Ibid.
13 Trudgen, 196.
14 Ibid.
15 Hill, *Broken Song*, 248.
16 Kaggwa, 'Is Reconciliation the New', 248–249.
17 San Roque, 165–166.
18 https://youtu.be/lOhw-4KJPd0
19 Transcribed by author from ibid.
20 https://youtu.be/birnA3_tm5E
21 Turner, *Lateline*, Jun 26, 2007; cited by Turner, P and Nicole Watson, 'The Trojan Horse.' In Altman and Hinkson, eds. *Coercive Reconciliation*. 2007:205.
22 Gaita, 'The Moral Force of Reconciliation.' In ibid, 295-306.
23 Ibid, 297.
24 Ibid, 305.

CHAPTER 10 – STILLING TERROR OF LOSS

> 'The Still' (Covid 19 page)
> 'You Are My Country' (RLS)
> 'Another Australia Day' (LDW)
> 'Love Can See in the Fog' (WS)

1 See interview by Paul Barclay accessible via https://www.abc.net.au/radionational/programs/bigideas/hugh-mackay-on-the-kindness-revolution/13423434
2 https://www.brainyquote.com/quotes/desmond_tutu_454129
3 Rose, *Nourishing Terrains*, 7; referencing the philosopher Levinas, in Hand, S. ed., 1989.
4 Ibid.
5 Ibid, 7–8.
6 Ibid, 10.
7 Ibid, 7; cited in Bruce, *The Longing*, Pre-Prologue as a quote.
8 Men and Women of Central Australia and Central Land Council, 7.
9 Bruce Breaden, ibid, 223–224.
10 Barbara Tjikatu, ibid, 228.
11 Check out Nakata, *Disciplining the Savages*, 2007.
12 A schema is 'a mental codification of experience that includes a particular organized way of perceiving cognitively and responding to a complex situation or set of stimuli' as defined by Merriam Webster Dictionary. https://www.merriam-webster.com
13 Bradley with *Yanyuwa* Families, Dedication.
14 Ibid, xiii.

15. MacKay, 2021:14.
16. It is interesting that *punu anangu* is translated as 'stem of a plant' in the following well-respected text: Goddard, 1992:6. One needs to take care in using this reference as an absolute however as language use can change.
17. O'Meara, 'Desert mourns as', Mar 8, 2017.
18. Ibid.
19. Bradley with *Yanyuwa* Families, 8.
20. This name is in the revived language of Tasmanian Aborigines called *palawa kani*. See http://tacinc.com.au/official-aboriginal-and-dual-names/
21. Power, 1999, 4-6.
22. 'There may be more to it!' is from a eulogy for a worker in this field of endeavour.
23. Fletcher, *Jesus and the*, 2013.

AFTERWORD

1. Hammarskyöld, *Markings*.
2. See Eppsteiner et al, 1998.
3. Personal communication with Cornell; see also assertion at the very beginning of his text *Dark Diamond*.
4. Hammarskyöld, *Markings*.
5. See http://holyirritant.blogspot.com/2010/05/cyril-hally-rip.html
6. Hally, 'Bicentennial Reflections', 12.
7. Ibid.
8. Ibid.
9. Ibid.
10. Cornell, 173.
11. Cunningham, 234.
12. Scott et al, 72.
13. See 'The Intervention' websites; some are: Anaya, James. *Report by the Special Rapporteur on the situation of human rights and fundamental freedoms of indigenous people – Situation of Indigenous People in Australia*, Jun 1, 2010. United Nations General Assembly, Human Rights Council Fifteenth session: A/ /15/37/Add.4; https://australianstogether.com.au/discover/the-wound-of-the-intervention; *World Council of Churches Living Letters Report*. http://www.ncca.org.au/files/Natsiec/2495_LivingLettersReport_BeyondIntervention_2010_f_lowres_r.pdf; *The Intervention*: Submission of the Human Rights and Equal Opportunity Commission (HREOC) to the Northern Territory Emergency Response Review Board on the Review of the Northern Territory Emergency Response Aug 15 2008. https://humanrights.gov.au/our-work/legal/northern-territory-emergency-response- review-board
14. Cox, in Scott et al, 195–211.
15. Ibid, 191.

NOTES

[16] See https://www.un.org/development/desa/indigenouspeoples/declaration-on-the-rights-of-indigenous-peoples
[17] Linda Mullett, *Kurnai* elder; cited in Mullett, Mullett and Leeson. 'An old place seen', 4.
[18] Mathnawi III, 2401–2405 in Helminski, 86.
[19] Wright, Alexis. In Scott et al, 244.

FURTHER ACKNOWLEDGEMENTS

[1] Cornell, 136.

REFLECTIONS

REFLECTIONS

TESSERAE KINNED

REFLECTIONS

www.ingramcontent.com/pod-product-compliance
Lightning Source LLC
Chambersburg PA
CBHW041306110526
44590CB00028B/4257